SELLING JESUS

by

Larry D. Rudder

Faith and Family Focus Series

RudderHaven
3014 Washington Ave
Granite City, IL 62040

Published by:
RudderHaven
3014 Washington Ave
Granite City, IL 62040
USA

First Softcover Printing, July 2016, RudderHaven
(978-1-932060-19-5)

Cover Design: Sheri L. Rudder

Printed in the United States of America

ISBN 978-1-932060-19-5

A Special Thanks. . . .

To the editors and publishers in my family who spent many hours preparing the manuscript for publication.

To my wife, Jeanette Rudder (M.A.), and my daughter, Dr. Cynthia K. Deatherage, for editing and proofing the complete manuscript.

To my son, Douglas, who prepared the manuscript for publication, including editing, layout, and design.

To my daughter-in-law, Sheri, who designed the cover art.

Contents

The Root of All Evil..1

False Profits...4

The Foolishness of Man..14

Pulling the Lever..34

Giving by Grace...39

Slain or Mesmerized...69

The Devil in the Works..79

Code Words or God's Word..86

The Commercialization of the Church...............................95

The Root of All Evil:

***For the love of money is the root of all evil: which while some coveted after, they have erred [strayed] from the faith, and pierced themselves through with many sorrows.* 1 Timothy 6:10**

What would you do if someone knocked at your door, and in tears said that she had lost her husband's paycheck? "He endorsed it and told me to deposit it in the bank, but I lost it."

"Do you want me to help you look for it?" I offered.

"No, that won't do any good," she responded.

"Well, then, why don't you call your husband and tell him to have a stop payment made on the check."

With that, she burst into full-blown tears. "I lost it all at the casino!"

"In that case," I said, "you'll have to tell him what happened and hope for the best."

I can't remember a time when so many people were caught up in a frenzy of fortune-seeking and greed. They buy unwanted magazines in hopes of being that one-in-fifteen-million subscribers to win instant wealth from Publishers' Clearing House.

How many people throw their money away on gambling—on what might seem trivial until they run into serious financial trouble? You know, things like lottery tickets, still hoping to be that one individual among multiplied millions of gamblers who think they can become millionaires overnight. After they add up their weekly losses, it begins to grow until they can't pay the power bill.

Then there's the fool who takes his annual trip to Las Vegas and burns a thousand dollars or more at the roulette tables or one-armed bandits. There's a reason they are called "bandits"! People who do these things are easy marks for anyone who offers them quick, easy money. They are looking for their pie-in-the-sky, and it always brings their downfall.

This folly has become so pervasive in our society that many Christians, or at least religious people, have bought into the same foolish behavior. But the root of their gambling problem doesn't rest in roulette wheels, lottery tickets, horse races, or card tables. It is a major project *hosted by churches* throughout the country, and the dealers are in our pulpits and on radio and television stations. Satan has invaded our churches with his demonic forces—forces that are so convincing that they are actually able to convince weak believers that what they offer comes directly from God!

It doesn't matter how often the religious gamblers in our churches are warned, they refuse to listen because they are wrapped up in the lust of the flesh. When a preacher stands in the pulpit delivering his or her get-rich-quick scheme, folks are ready to be hooked into swallowing the bait—including the hook, line, and sinker. 2 Corinthians 11:13–15 describes these pulpit charlatans in no uncertain terms: "For such are false apostles, deceitful workers, transforming themselves into the apostles of Christ. And no marvel; for Satan himself is transformed into an angel of light. Therefore it is no great thing if his ministers be transformed as ministers of righteousness, whose end shall be according to their works."

These false prophets are demon-driven and are able to twist the Scriptures in such a way as to be extremely convincing to those people who are riding the storm between their faith and their flesh. They are led by the same serpent who led Adam and Eve astray. If you are one of those who have chosen to follow these "snake-oil" preachers, remember their "end shall be according to their works."

I would exhort you not to put this book away until you have given it an honest reading. It could save you from bankruptcy, divorce, and serious judgment from Almighty God!

False Profits:

Riches profit not in the day of wrath: but righteousness delivereth from death**. [Proverbs 11:4]**

"Then one of the twelve, called Judas Iscariot, went unto the chief priests, and said unto them, What will ye give me, and I will deliver [Jesus] unto you? And they covenanted with him for thirty pieces of silver" (Matthew 26:14–15). Things haven't changed with the passing of Judas Iscariot. People are still selling out our Lord for that old filthy lucre. But let me warn you, you can't do a thing with your riches while the world burns, and your eternal Judge sits on His throne to determine your eternal destiny, and that time is fast approaching.

Building up our earthly treasures doesn't amount to a pile of meadow muffins when time is running out. As Paul wrote to Timothy, "But godliness with contentment is great gain. For we brought nothing into this world, and it is certain that we can carry nothing out" (1 Timothy 6:6–7).

That's why Paul told Timothy to "charge them that are rich in this world, that they be not highminded" (verse 17). Have you noticed the press coverage of the rich and famous who continually break the law and use their fame and fortune to get them off the hook? It matters not what the judge might say. They will continue to behave in antisocial ways because they always seem to get away with their bad behavior. But when these same cultural snobs face the only Judge whose decision is final and irrevocable, they won't have a thing to laugh about.

They won't be able to pay cold cash to get away with their evil deeds, nor will their fame be of any value.

Time is the issue for such people—time to review their spiritual condition and realize that they can't "trust in uncertain riches." In verse 17, they are also told to trust "in the living God." That's why we are warned in Romans 13:11, "And that knowing the time, that now it is high time to awake out of sleep: for now is our salvation nearer than when we believed."

The church of the last days, the fallen church, wants everyone to believe that it is a vibrant, Christ-honoring organization, but nothing could be further from the truth. Those who speak for that church only seek to fulfill their own vanity, their own aggrandizement. They lust after wealth, pleasure, and power here and now. Sad to say, this is the dominant church of today— known in the Book of Revelation as the church of the Laodiceans.

There was a vast difference between the historic churches where Jonathan Edwards, George Whitefield, John Wesley, and Charles Hadden Spurgeon preached and the worldly mega-churches of today. Their churches were on fire for Jesus Christ. Their only goals were to reach the lost for Christ and edify the body of believers by declaring the Gospel of salvation and the anointing of the Holy Spirit in their worship. There was no entertainment of any kind. Spurgeon would allow neither a choir nor an organ in his Metropolitan Tabernacle. You see, their ultimate goal was to preach Christ and Him crucified and risen.

Unlike Spurgeon, I think an organ can do a lot to uplift the worship in any church, and I love a good spirit-filled choir, but I'm afraid the Holy Spirit is not at work in many churches today. As we readily see, today's churches disallow the Holy Spirit's leadership, choosing rather to entertain in order to draw a crowd. A few of them still preach a good message, but their tactics fall far short of the holiness that God requires of His people. The majority are not only entertainment oriented, but they are steeped in the satanic doctrine of seed theology, often called *the health and wealth movement*. Their churches are built on greed.

In Revelation 3:16–19, Jesus said, "So then because thou art lukewarm, and neither cold nor hot, I will spue [*vomit*] thee out of my mouth. Because thou sayest, I am rich, and increased with goods, and have need of nothing; and knowest not that thou art wretched, and miserable, and poor, and blind, and naked: I counsel thee to buy of me gold tried in the fire, that thou mayest be rich; and white raiment, that thou mayest be clothed, and that the shame of thy nakedness do not appear; and anoint thine eyes with eyesalve, that thou mayest see. As many as I love, I rebuke and chasten: be zealous therefore, and repent."

The Lord Jesus Christ spoke these words to the church at Laodicea. He warns that their lust for money will be their downfall unless they turn to the only one who can bring them hope for eternity. Gold tried in the fire is pure gold—a gold that can't be found on Earth—such as that which comprises the city of gold, the new heavenly Jerusalem. Revelation 21:18 describes it: "And the building of the wall of it was of jasper: and the city was *pure* gold, like unto clear glass."

The Laodicean denomination demands everything from God. It is a "gimme" church. "Gimme my money now! Gimme my miracles now! Gimme excitement! Gimme everything I want, and do it now!" There is very little thanksgiving on their part. After all, they hold the view that everything is rightfully theirs.

There are many things that will turn the heads of people who feign religiosity in these evil days, the chief of which is money. It blinds the eyes of those who lust after it, and the only eye-salve that can cure their blindness is that of the Holy Spirit. They give only to get. Let this be a warning to those who have their blinders on and think they will profit from the Lord through religious giving—God will rebuke and chastise you unless you repent!

Seed Theology is the main doctrine of that church. This is the telltale sign of the Laodiceans, and it makes the Lord Jesus Christ sick to His stomach—so much so that it makes Him want to vomit according to Revelation 3:16.

It is one of the many false doctrines that Satan has used to lure many new believers who listen to the false prophets of this age, issues that cause young Christians to stumble, to question their new-found faith, and to distract them from the one great goal that lies ahead—"the mark for the prize of the high calling of God in Christ Jesus" (Philippians 3:14).

At the same time, seasoned Christians are not completely immune to these destructive ideas. When some people hear that somehow they are going to get their share of the "pie in the sky" a little early, the old flesh gets the best of them, and they are quick to jump on the proverbial bandwagon, hoping for a quick and easy method of getting God to open the windows of Heaven for them and rain down earthly wealth. Sorry, it doesn't work that way. Those ideas are designed by Satan, and that kind of wealth belongs only to him.

People in this present generation, and especially in America, are more susceptible to buying into this insidious doctrine because we are the wealthiest generation in the history of the world. We are so used to having *things* that our appetites for more things are out of control in spite of the fact that, as of this writing, we are experiencing a recession. Politicians tell us that we are coming out of it, but they will customarily say anything to protect their jobs and drive us deeper into debt. We may, in fact, face a depression greater than the Great Depression of years gone by.

Our recession hasn't quenched the thirst for more and more things. Our government is taking more from the taxpayers, spending more on wasteful projects, and sinking our nation into an abyss of debt that we will never crawl out of. In fact, many economists believe this country is destined to economic self-destruction—an ultimate financial collapse. Still we buy things we don't need, spending as though we have a bottomless pit of money—mostly by putting it all on credit cards that will eventually bankrupt us. If that doesn't happen because of our unbridled spending habits, it will be the result of computer hackers who break into store computers or identity thieves who will take everything we own.

When I was a youngster, my family was viewed as better off than the rest of my neighborhood because we had an indoor toilet and a real bathtub. Our neighbors still had outhouses in their backyards and wash tubs in their kitchens for bathing. Today's families spend more money on their bathrooms than we did on our houses.

People feel cheated if they can't afford a gigantic high definition color television with a recording device to guarantee they don't miss anything and surround-sound to add to the noise. People today spend more for a car than I did for my house and two city lots in the 1970s. I had to give up the house, selling it for what I owed on it, when I entered the evangelistic ministry. People weep when they have trouble buying a luxurious house, when throughout my ministry I couldn't afford a house at all (not even to rent), and our family, including my wife and three children, was content. But you see, we followed the disciples' examples by selling everything we had and going on the road to serve the Lord. We were only able to raise enough money to buy a used van that was often used for sleeping, a small utility trailer for our basic needs and ministry equipment—and that is even more than the disciples had as they went on the road in obedience to our Lord!

I've heard couples complain that it takes two people to earn a living these days, but that is only true because of their insatiable appetite for more and higher quality *stuff*. If they would stop and reason out what it is that they *need* to live on rather than what they *want* to make their lives more comfortable and entertaining, surrendering their hedonistic values to the will of Almighty God, they would quickly find that they could live on a whole lot less and have more time to serve the Lord Jesus Christ as they are commanded to do.

You see, religious people are so determined to make their lives as comfortable and self-satisfying as possible that they leave very little time or desire, if any, to meet their responsibilities to Almighty God. Until they change their value system from that of the world and the flesh to one that is truly spiritual and Christ-honoring, their addiction to temporal wealth will continue. More important than that, they would not be so susceptible to caving in to those evil teachers of a theology of greed—false prophets who can't keep their hands out of other peoples' pockets.

Can a lifestyle without all of the luxuries people think they need be practical? Absolutely! My wife and I have no credit cards and never will have. We don't ask for credit. If we think we will need anything, we save up for it–including setting aside money for emergencies. If we can't pay for it, we don't need it! You see, we have learned the Scriptural admonition "to be content with such things as we have." Paul warns us in Romans 13:8 to "owe no man any thing, but to love one another," and he practiced what he preached. He said of himself in Philippians 4:11–13, "I have learned, in whatsoever state I am, therewith to be content. I know both how to be abased, and I know how to abound: every where and in all things I am instructed both to be full and to be hungry, both to abound and to suffer need. I can do all things through Christ which strengtheneth me."

He warned Timothy about those who would convince us otherwise calling them "men of corrupt minds, and destitute of the truth, supposing that gain is godliness: from such withdraw thyself. But godliness with contentment is great gain. For we brought nothing into this world, and it is certain we can carry nothing out. And having food and raiment let us be therewith content" (1 Timothy 6:5–8). That leaves no room at all for the things that people today think they need to fulfill their fleshly desires. Many church members today are Christians in name only. I dare say they would rather burn their Bibles than to do what God tells them in His Word.

If you don't heed these Biblical admonitions, you will soon learn what Proverbs 22:7 means: "The rich ruleth over the poor, and the borrower is servant to the lender." If you don't think that's true, try skipping your payments. Hebrews 13:5 reminds us, "Let your conversation [mode of living] be without covetousness; and be content with such things as ye have: for he hath said, I will never leave thee, nor forsake thee."

There are many charlatans in today's pulpits who have devised a grand scheme to bilk zealous believers out of their hard-earned money by appealing to their "old man," the carnal nature of the flesh. These pulpiteers of the Laodicean church have created a "doctrine" of their own and twisted the Scriptures to convince people that what they are doing is of God. As I said previously, their doctrine is best known as *Seed Theology*, and they base it on Galatians 6:7, telling us "for whatsoever a man soweth, that shall he also reap." This theology is based entirely on avarice or greed and the power that accompanies it. I prefer to call it *Greed Theology*. They argue that, by your giving to their ministry (or, as they say, "to the Lord"), you will receive a like reward multiplied a hundred times. Of course, they can prove that their doctrine works because they are all rich! Unfortunately, if they hadn't scammed their followers out of their money, these preachers wouldn't be wealthy.

These scams are typified by such promotions as an anointed handkerchief that will cause you to miraculously become filthy rich if you send your money to the filthy rich preacher, who promises to send you his magic cloth along with a medallion inscribed with words like "How to become wealthy." Then there is the program that begins with a tap dancing, expensively garbed "singer," whose only words are occasional "hallelujahs," while the camera masterfully displays his fancy clothes and expensive shoes. When this long production of worldly exhibitionism is finished, the cameras pan to the TV preacher who is telling the television audience how much wealth the Lord is going to reward them with because of their generosity in sending the preacher their money. What will he use it for? If he is typical, he will buy more fancy clothes, jewelry, designer shoes, expensive automobiles, a jet airplane, luxurious office buildings and furnishings, personal property and real estate that neither you nor I could ever afford—and I promise you by the Word of Almighty God that you *will not* be rewarded for your generous offerings!

I have often become a target of greed preachers in the mail that I receive, promising me great wealth if I purchase their prayer cloths, beads, books, oil, and countless other devices and gimmicks. Recently I received a letter assuring me that God would clear away all of my bills (which I carefully avoid accumulating) and bring me great riches if I bought a particular book and followed its advice. In days gone by, these gimmicks were referred to as "snake oil," but desperate people in today's economy are willing to grasp at anything they think might possibly reverse their financial plight into one of riches and easy living. That's the very attitude that causes people to become addicted to buying lottery tickets, entering sweepstakes, and visiting gambling casinos in hopes of getting rich the easy way—often losing their paychecks to their futile lust for money. I've a message for followers of the greed preachers. It doesn't work that way!

Satan has been able to blind the eyes of many religious people by appealing to their lust for money. Have you noticed that more and more "Prosperity Conferences" are being advertised and fewer revivals and evangelistic meetings, especially among those television preachers and others who are caught up in the greed theology explosion? How many times does one of these preachers refer to gaining wealth or prosperity in his or her sermon—a sermon that *should* be concerned with the salvation of lost souls and/or the exhortation of believers?

Remember, if it isn't in the Bible, it is just a gimmick used by those who would grab your money and run. They are charlatans from the word *go*. These are men and women without conscience. They have sold out to the devil and the root of all evil.

The Foolishness of Man:

***O full of subtilty and all mischief, thou child of the devil, thou enemy of all righteousness, wilt thou not cease to pervert the right ways of the Lord?* [Acts 13:10]**

In this section, we will use the same Scriptures to show how these purveyors of greed have turned the Word of God into a lie for their own greedy and selfish purposes and have seduced others into believing this dastardly lie. Be forewarned by 1 Timothy 4:1–2, “Now the Spirit speaketh expressly, that in the latter times some shall depart from the faith, giving heed to *seducing* spirits, and doctrines of devils; Speaking lies in hypocrisy; having their *conscience seared with a hot iron.*” In other words, they have lied so often that they have learned to believe their own lies, and they use those lies to fleece people who are easily fooled.

I suppose the best illustration I can give is that of a preacher from Chicago, Robb Thompson, who stated on the Trinity Broadcasting Network (TBN), a leading proponent of greed theology (as are most so-called Christian television networks) on May 31, 2005, “Money is the vehicle through which God performs His will.” This is the kind of teaching we hear from the “Winning in Life” broadcast. According to Mr. Thompson’s statement, if there were no money, God could not perform His will. There would be no salvation for anyone!

I wonder how a man could make such a statement in the light of Hebrews 9:14 where we see that the precious blood of Jesus Christ is declared to be the vehicle through which God performs His will: "How much more shall the blood of Christ, who through the eternal Spirit offered himself without spot to God, purge your conscience from dead works to serve the living God?"

In Hebrews 10:9, our Lord said, "Lo, I come to do thy will, O God. He taketh away the first [testament or covenant], that he may establish the second."

The writer of Hebrews continues in verse 10, "By the which [or by whose] will we are sanctified through the offering of the body of Jesus Christ once for all."

What gall! What sheer sacrilege to replace the blood of Jesus Christ with the filthy lucre of the world's making! While the love of money is the root of all evil, the blood of Christ is the absolute expression of God's will and God's love.

Regarding these false prophets, Paul said in 2 Corinthians 11:13–15: "For such are false apostles, deceitful workers, transforming themselves into the apostles of Christ. And no marvel; for Satan himself is transformed into an angel of light. Therefore it is no great thing if his ministers also be transformed as the ministers of righteousness; whose end shall be according to their works."

When I was a new Christian at the age of seventeen, I was invited to be a "personal worker" at a tent meeting in my home town. I had no idea what a personal worker was at the time but later learned that it is the same as a *counselor*. In other words, when a person walks down the aisle in an evangelistic meeting in response to an invitation to commit his life to Christ, a personal worker is supposed to step out and meet that person, with a Bible or other material in hand, to answer questions, pray with, and give Scriptural guidance to that individual.

At that time, I had no idea how to do any of those things because I was a brand new Christian myself with very little knowledge of the Scriptures. However, in my experience with this particular evangelist, the personal workers didn't really need to know anything at all about the Bible or to be able to pray with or counsel anyone. Instead, the evangelist called us all together under the tent to instruct us in the art of raising money for him. We were told that when he announced that it was time for the audience to get up from their seats and march around the perimeter of the tent in order to drop their offerings in the huge barrels that rested at each side of the pulpit, it was our responsibility as personal workers to make a point of taking a twenty-dollar bill from our wallets or purses, hold the currency high so that everyone could see what was expected of them, and drop the money in the barrels. At that time, a twenty-dollar bill was comparable to a hundred dollar bill today!

This preacher was one who used an almost hypnotic approach by speaking with a heavy whisper into his microphone. He would say things like, "You don't think you can afford to give to the Lord? My friend, you can't afford *not* to. When you give to the Lord, He promises to give it back to you a hundredfold. That's right! You 'give, and it shall be given unto you; good measure, pressed down, and shaken together, and running over.'" The preacher quoted only a part of Luke 6:38.

What the man failed to do was to explain that Jesus was talking about relationships between people, that is, people will treat you the way you treat them. The last sentence in verse 38 says, "For with the *same* measure that ye meet withal it shall be measured to you again." If the verse is talking about money—there goes the hundredfold return (one hundred times what you give). What it does say is that if we give generously to the poor (not to the preacher), we will have the same generosity shown to us. It is the same context that tells us to "give to every man that asketh of thee; and of him that taketh away thy goods ask them not again" (verse 30). In other words, don't expect anything in return. Verse 36 tells us, "Be ye therefore merciful, as your Father also is merciful" (verse 36).

In verses 45–46, Jesus said, "A good man out of the good *treasure of his heart* bringeth forth that which is good; and an evil man out of the *evil treasure of his heart* bringeth forth that which is evil: for of *the abundance of the heart* his mouth speaketh. And why call ye me, Lord, Lord, and do not the things which I say?"

When we study the Scriptures, we must always keep each verse in its context with the rest of the passage. In the case of Luke 6:38, the quotation is from Christ's Sermon on the Mount, an oft-quoted chapter from the New Testament. In this sermon, Jesus is telling His Jewish followers how they must treat each other if they expect to be treated well themselves. Where financial rewards are concerned, Jesus said in verse 23, "Rejoice ye in that day, and leap for joy: for, behold, your reward is great *in heaven.*"

In the very next verse, He said, "But woe unto you that are rich! for ye have received your consolation." Where the believer is concerned, every time riches or treasures are mentioned in the New Testament, it is always in the context of our *heavenly* rewards. Any other reference to wealth pertains to unbelievers and is speaking about earthly riches that drag the lost to hell and cost the saved their heavenly rewards.

In Isaiah 53:9, the prophet writes about Christ's death: "And he made his grave *with the wicked*, and *with the rich* in his death; because he had done no violence, neither was any deceit in his mouth."

Luke 6:24 simply tells us that those who place their trust in wealth on earth will have no eternal treasure. Their place in eternity has been determined by where they placed their trust in this life. In verse 34, our Lord told those on that mountainside, "And if ye lend [or *give*] to them of whom ye hope to receive, what thank have ye? For sinners also lend to sinners, to receive as much again." Jesus is simply saying, "Don't give to anyone with the intention of receiving anything back. You have only done the right thing, and you shouldn't expect to receive any reward. That's what sinners do!"

Therefore, don't listen to anyone who tells you that giving money to his cause will bring you some financial reward in return. It's a lie! (Notice that such a person always tells us that giving to *him* is the same as giving to *the Lord*.) However, there is a basic principle given in verse 31. It is commonly called *the Golden Rule*: "And as ye would that men should do to you, do ye also to them likewise." The way we usually hear it expressed is, "Do unto others as you would have them do unto you." That expresses the complete context of Christ's Sermon on the Mount, and there is not the slightest hint that you will receive multiplied returns on your money by giving to the preacher, or to the television program, or for that matter, to the church. Any rewards you will receive will be waiting for you *in Heaven.* That is what is meant in verse 35, "But love ye your enemies, and do good, and lend [*give*], hoping for *nothing* again; and your reward shall be great, and ye shall be the children of the Highest."

The reference to "a hundredfold" is taken from Mark 10:29–30, and when I say *taken from*, I mean that quite literally. It is taken completely out of context. Let's read the verse: "And Jesus answered and said, Verily I say unto you, There is no man that hath left house [literally, *household* or *family*], or brethren, or sisters, or father, or mother, or wife, or children, or lands, for my sake, and the gospel's, But he shall receive an hundredfold now in this time, houses, and brethren, and sisters, and mothers, and children, and lands, with persecutions; and in the world to come eternal life."

Take note, first of all, that the person referred to is leaving his family, including brothers, sisters, children, father and mother, in order to go out and preach the gospel—not giving money to a television evangelist or anyone else. There is absolutely no reference to money or material wealth! Then note that this person will receive a hundredfold "houses [again, literally, *households* or *families*], brothers, sisters, mothers, children, and lands, with persecutions; and in the world to come eternal life."

For clarity, let me repeat that in plain terms. First, ask yourself what the *hundredfold* refers to, and remember that a hundredfold means one hundred times what you gave up. You will receive a hundred households, a hundred brothers, a hundred sisters, a hundred mothers, a hundred children, a hundred lands, and a hundred persecutions!

Once again, there is no reference at all to receiving money or any other worldly wealth. What the person *is* promised are persecutions on earth and eternal life in Heaven.

Jesus did not say, "I am come that they might have money or other material wealth and that they might have money more abundantly." No! He said, "I am come that they might have *life*, and that they might have it [*life*] more abundantly" (John 10:10).

The Greek word for life (*zoe*) in this context is just that—life—that which bears the mind and soul. There is no reference at all to attaining material riches in this life.

According to Mark 10:29–30, what happens when you are adopted into the family of God, as stated in Romans 8:15, is that you are immediately surrounded by others in the family who become your brothers and sisters, even mothers, in the faith. And when you preach the gospel and win others to a saving knowledge of Christ, they are also adopted into the family—your children in the faith. Note, however, that there is no mention of any other father in this context. That is because God Himself is the Father of all who believe. But when you take such a strong stand for the gospel you will suffer persecutions in this life.

In Luke 8:21, when the disciples brought Jesus' mother and brothers to him, saying that they wished to see Him, He answered, "My mother and my brethren are *these* which *hear the word of God, and do it.*" In other words, they are those who have the gospel preached to them and receive it by confessing Christ as their Lord.

The word "lands" in Mark 10:30 refers to *fields* or

pastures. Jesus said in John 4:35–36: “Say not ye, There are yet four months, and then cometh harvest? behold, I say unto you, Lift up your eyes, and look on the fields [*lands*]; for they are white already to harvest. And he that reapeth receiveth wages [heavenly rewards], and gathereth fruit unto life eternal [saved souls]: that both he that soweth and he that reapeth may rejoice together.”

Those are the same “lands” or fields referred to in Mark 10! You see, the “hundredfold” refers to *saved souls*, not money returned on financial investments as the charlatans would lead you to believe! That is why the hundredfold are won “with persecutions.”

In 1 Timothy 6:5, Paul warns us not to be deceived by “perverse disputings of men of corrupt minds, and destitute of the truth, supposing that *gain* is godliness: from such *withdraw thyself*.”

Then he adds in verses 6–10: “But godliness with *contentment* is great gain. For we brought nothing into this world, and it is certain we can carry nothing out. And having food and raiment let us *be therewith content*. But they that will be rich fall into temptation and a snare, and into many foolish and hurtful lusts, which drown men in destruction and perdition. For the love of money is the root of all evil: which while some coveted after, they have *erred* [been seduced] from the faith, and pierced themselves through with many sorrows.”

I recently heard a young greed preacher on television try to use the rich young ruler who came to Jesus asking what he could do to inherit eternal life to show how angry unbelievers get when confronted with spiritual matters. The preacher said that the answer Jesus gave regarding five of the ten commandments caused the rich young ruler to angrily break off the conversation and stomp away in frustration. What the TV preacher failed to say was that the young man turned away after Jesus told him to sell all that he had, give it to the poor, take up the cross, and follow Christ. You see the greed preacher could not complete the Scripture analogy without refuting his own greedy belief system. What drove off the young ruler was not Christ's insistence upon his keeping the ten commandments but rather His insistence that the man surrender his worldly goods to the poor, *taking up the cross*, and following in the footsteps of Jesus!

Mark 10 does indeed tell about a young Jewish man who came running to Jesus to ask what he could do to inherit eternal life. When Jesus told him to keep the law, the young man replied that he had done so from his youth. At that point, the Scripture tells us: "Then Jesus beholding him loved him, and said unto him, One thing thou lackest: go thy way, sell whatsoever thou hast, and give to the poor, and thou shalt have treasure in heaven: and come, take up the cross, and follow me. And he was sad at *that* [italics mine] saying, and went away grieved: for he had great possessions. And Jesus looked around about, and saith unto his disciples, How hardly shall they that have riches enter into the kingdom of God! And the disciples were astonished at his words. But Jesus answereth again, and saith unto them, Children, how hard is it for them that trust in riches to enter into the kingdom of God! It is easier for a camel to go through the eye of a needle, than for a rich man to enter into the kingdom of God."

Those who preach their heresies never ask you to sell your possessions and give the money to the poor. They want your money for themselves, so they can continue their high-rolling lifestyles. They never tell you to take up the cross and follow Christ. I've watched hundreds of hours of greed programming, and these money worshipers always tell you to give up your money and follow *them.*

Sadly, the avaricious preachers of greed theology who have erred from the faith also use Psalm 37:4 to show that God will give you anything you want: "Delight thyself also in the Lord; and he shall give thee the desires of thine heart." They ignore the fact that the Old Testament was written for Israel, a nation of people whose hope was and is in the land in which they live—the Holy Land. That is where their kingdom is and where their holy places are. That is where the throne of David was, but today's Israel does not comprehend the spiritual throne of David and our spiritual Holy Land. The Christian's kingdom is called Heaven and eventually the New Earth—not this earth as some of today's errant prophecy preachers insist—so the promises of prosperity for Israel have nothing at all to do with the Christian's prosperity today.

Indeed, as with the patriarchs of old, we are called "strangers and pilgrims" on this earth, people who are looking for "a better country" (Hebrews 11:13–16). Our prosperity is what is laid up for us in the kingdom of God and of Christ—a spiritual treasure that far surpasses the pitiful wealth of this world.

Psalm 37, however, does not speak about material or financial prosperity that those who would con you out of your money want you to believe. The first two verses exhort Israel not to be envious of evil doers who seem to prosper in this life, because they will lose it all in the end, but verse 3 tells us to "Trust in the Lord, and *do good*; so shalt thou dwell in the land, and verily thou shalt be fed." Delighting yourself in the Lord does not convey the slightest hint of giving away money to some elitist who likes to follow the life of a high-roller.

As Christians our heavenly rewards result from the good works that we do, not the money that we invest or give away. It springs from that common partnership of faith and good works that James spoke of in his epistle. In James 2:15–17, he said: "If a brother or sister be naked, and destitute of daily food, And one of you say unto them, Depart in peace, be ye warmed and filled; notwithstanding ye give them not those things which are needful to the body; what doth it profit? Even so faith, if it hath not works, is dead, being alone."

Notice that the verses do not instruct the destitute to first give their last pennies to the ministry of some errant preacher in order for God to bless them in return. They simply instruct those who have something to give just to *give it* to those who need it.

Ephesians 4:28 is quite clear about how Christians are to live, "Let him that stole steal no more: but rather let him labour, working with his hands the thing which is good, that he may have to give to him that needeth." Good, honest work is what is required for us to earn our wages, not the casting of coins into some ethereal "lottery of life." Those wages are to be earned not only to meet our own needs but also to provide for the needs of others—not for amassing a fortune in financial rewards as a result of our religious giving.

In 1 John 3:17 we are told, "But whoso hath this

world's good, and seeth his brother have need, and shutteth up his bowels of compassion from him, how dwelleth the love of God in him?"

That is the theme of Psalm 37. "The wicked borroweth, and payeth not again; but the righteous sheweth mercy, and giveth" (verse 21).

When it comes to wealth, verse 16 says, "A little that a righteous man hath is better than the riches of many wicked."

What, then, is verse 4 telling us? Let's look at it again, "Delight thyself also in the Lord; and he shall give thee the desires of thine heart." In order to apply this verse in a personal way, we must understand the word *delight* in the original Hebrew: *anag*, which means *to be pliable*. Once again, we recognize the Lordship of Christ as we allow ourselves to be pliable to His leadership. How do we delight ourselves?—*in the Lord*, not in money or any other worldly thing. Delighting ourselves in God has absolutely nothing to do with personal gain or money. It has to do only with our willingness to obey Him.

Then we must ask ourselves what it is that we desire with our hearts. Do our desires rest in those earthly treasures that we will leave behind when we die? Do they rest in those treasures that cause us to do evil things and build up worldly possessions? Or do the desires of our hearts reflect what Jesus said in Matthew 6:19–21, "Lay not up for yourselves treasures upon earth, where moth and rust doth corrupt, and where thieves break through and steal: But lay up for yourselves treasures *in heaven*, where neither moth nor rust doth corrupt, and where thieves do not break through nor steal: For *where your treasure is, there will your heart be also*."

Is your heart in Heaven with our Lord or on earth with the prince of the power of the air—the devil? Clearly, if we are to delight ourselves in obeying the Lord, then the desires of our hearts are doing those things that please Him—the direct results of our pliability to His leadership.

Finally, if we examine Galatians 6:7, the first greed theology proof text that we saw, we can see where these greedy theologians have misled people. The whole verse says, "Be not deceived; God is not mocked: for whatsoever a man soweth, that shall he also reap." Obviously, this verse is talking about *evil behavior* rather than money. *Good* behavior does not deceive anyone, nor does it mock God!

If we read on, however, verses 8–10 tell us: "For he that soweth to his flesh [lives to satisfy his carnal nature] shall of the flesh reap corruption [or *destruction*]; but he that soweth to the Spirit [walks in the Spirit, serving the Lord] shall of the Spirit reap life everlasting. And let us not be weary in well doing: for in due season we shall reap, if we faint not. As we have therefore opportunity, let us do good unto all men, especially unto them who are of the household of faith."

As we have seen in previous references, the rewards we receive for eternity are earned in this life according to our works, whether good or bad. When we live after the flesh, we will suffer not just in this present life but in the day of judgment. Likewise, when we do the works of God, we will see the fruits of our works in this life, but our rewards are laid up for us in the kingdom of Heaven.

I have on several occasions heard preachers say that "whatsoever a man soweth, that shall he also reap" means that if you sow money, you will reap money. If you sow land, you will reap land. That is not what the verse says at all! Clearly, if you sow to the flesh, you will not get more fleshly things. No! Look again at what the Bible says! If you sow to the flesh, you will "reap *corruption* or *destruction*." If you sow to the Spirit, will you not reap more Spirit? No! You will reap "life everlasting." What the verse is teaching is that you will receive the appropriate eternal reward or punishment for your behavior.

No single Bible verse stands alone. A doctrine cannot be built on one verse of Scripture! It must always be kept in its context. Furthermore, we must also check not only the immediate context of a verse but also compare it to the context of the rest of the Bible.

For example, James 4:9 says, "Be afflicted, and mourn, and weep: let your laughter be turned to mourning, and your joy to heaviness." Does that mean that Christians are supposed to be unhappy, grieving wretches? Of course not, but there have been churches that have taught that concept, causing their followers to be stern, self-abasing individuals! If we read it in context, we find that the preceding verse exhorts, "Draw nigh to God, and he will draw nigh to you. Cleanse your hands, ye sinners; and purify your hearts, ye double minded." And the verse that comes after it says, "Humble yourselves in the sight of the Lord, and he shall lift you up."

In other words, those who are wicked, double-minded sinners should mourn their wicked behavior. They have no reason to laugh or be unburdened until their burdens are lifted by purifying their hearts and humbling themselves to Almighty God.

In essence, that is what happens when we quote a verse out of context. That is also true when we use a verse, even in its immediate context, without comparing it to the context of the rest of the Bible.

When it comes to our Christian giving, if our desire is to build up our material wealth in this life, then our hearts are not in the right place. We are still in the flesh and not in the Spirit. Always remember that God is concerned with what is in your heart, not what is in your pocket. If riches were to be had through our giving to the church or giving to another ministry, the disciples would have been the wealthiest men in the world rather than the poorest, but their wealth was garnered in the treasuries of Heaven and not in this life.

Jesus told his disciples in Luke 12:28–34: "If then God so clothe the grass, which is today in the field, and tomorrow is cast into the oven; how much more will he clothe you, O ye of little faith? And seek not ye what ye shall eat, or what ye shall drink, neither be ye of doubtful mind. For all these things do the nations of the world seek after; and your Father knoweth that ye have need of these things. But rather seek ye the kingdom of God; and all these things shall be added unto you. Fear not, little flock; for it is your Father's good pleasure to give you the kingdom. Sell that ye have, and give alms [*give to the poor*]; provide yourselves bags which wax not old, a *treasure in the heavens* that faileth not, where no thief approacheth, neither moth corrupteth. For where your treasure is, there will your heart be also."

I heard one of the greed preachers boasting that the part of verse 31 saying, "and all these things shall be added unto you," means *all* these things. The woman was trying to stretch the verse to include "the desires of our hearts" or whatever we want. She failed to remind her audience that the "all" referred to clothing, food, and drink—the necessities of life.

The men whom God chose to put His word into written form and spread the gospel throughout their world were among the poorest men on earth. As we have seen in Luke 9, they went out into the world with one coat, no money, no food, a staff, and one pair of sandals. They sold all of their earthly possessions and gave them away. They were jailed, and they were tortured. They gave their all—including their lives. According to the greed theologians, the disciples should have been the wealthiest men on earth! Or as one greed preacher screamed on his television show, "You are children of the King! Act like it!" But the disciples died in poverty. Paul spent his last days as a prisoner; and John, who penned the last book of the Bible, died while in exile on the Isle of Patmos.

How dare such self-aggrandizing charlatans elevate themselves above those early disciples—men who gave everything they had to serve the Lord Jesus Christ and, in turn, lost their lives in total poverty as they fulfilled their commitments!

Even the Apostle Paul knew what it meant to surrender everything to Christ. He wrote from prison to the Church at Philippi: "Brethren, be followers together of me, and mark [Greek: *take aim at* or *watch out for*] them which walk so as ye have us for an ensample. (For many walk, of whom I have told you often, and now tell you even weeping, that they are *the enemies of the cross of Christ*: Whose end is destruction, whose God is their belly, and whose glory is in their shame, who mind *earthly things*)" (Philippians 3:17–19).

Paul warns us to be on guard against those who dwell among us but who fail to follow the examples of the apostles—those who are the enemies of the cross of Christ. They are easily spotted by their fleshly exploits, their unending appetites for earthly or worldly things, who glory in their disgraceful behavior. These are doomed to destruction. They pretend to be followers of Christ, but their true identities are divulged by their attempts at amassing worldly wealth. In Philippians 4:11–13, he added: "Not that I speak in respect of want: for I have learned, in whatsoever state I am, therewith to be content. I know both how to be abased, and I know how to abound: every where and in all things I am instructed both to be full and to be hungry, both to abound and to suffer need. I can do all things through Christ, which strengtheneth me."

But Paul was in prison and grateful for the supplies that were sent to him by the church at Philippi. He gives them the assurance that "my God shall supply all your *need* according to his riches in glory by Christ Jesus" (verse 19). I must repeat that there is a vast difference between your *needs* and your *wants*. You need clothes, but you don't need designer clothing. You need a place in which to dwell, but you don't need a $500,000 house. No one needs diamonds and other expensive jewelry. You may need a means of getting to your job, but you don't need a new luxury car. The church at Philippi, as poor as it was, shared a portion of their poverty with impoverished Paul.

Above all, Jesus Himself, best illustrates the fact that

giving does not guarantee financial returns. He said in Luke 9:58, "Foxes have holes, and birds of the air have nests; but the Son of man hath not where to lay his head." Ask yourself this: "Am I better than Jesus Christ?"

In Luke 4:18–19, He said: "The Spirit of the Lord is upon me, because he hath anointed me to preach the gospel to the poor; he hath sent me to heal the brokenhearted, to preach deliverance to the captives, and recovering of sight to the blind, to set at liberty them that are bruised, To preach the acceptable year of the Lord."

Did you notice what was missing? There was no reference at all to financial rewards. Jesus did *not say*, "and to preach the rewards of great wealth through giving." Jesus did not come for that purpose and *never* promised or inferred such an obscene notion!

The most important truth that we must recognize is this: Giving money or any other material thing to the church or any other ministry will not gain anyone an inch toward Heaven or the treasures thereof. You might ask, "But what about the widow's mite? Didn't she receive a reward?" Well, let's look at it in Luke 21:1–6: "And he looked up, and saw the rich men casting their gifts into the treasury. And he saw also a certain poor widow casting in thither two mites [*the value of a penny*]. And he said, Of a truth I say unto you, that this poor widow hath cast in more than they all: For all these have of their abundance cast in unto the offerings of God: but she of her penury hath cast in all the living that she had. And as some spake of the temple, how it was adorned with goodly stones and gifts, he said, As for these things which ye behold, the days will come, in the which there shall not be left one stone upon another, that shall not be thrown down."

First, the rich men gave a considerable sum of money, but there is no mention at all of their receiving anything in return. In fact, the Lord held them in scorn.

Second, the widow gave two mites, all that she had to her name, and the Lord said that her gift was superior to theirs—but still there was no mention of rewards in this life. Why? Because her treasures were laid up in Heaven. That's where her heart was.

Finally, some who were with Him pointed out that the temple was a costly building, obviously inferring that it took a lot of money to build and maintain it. Sound familiar? Isn't that what you are told about building and maintaining expensive church property today? But what did Jesus say? In effect, His response was, "So what? It has no spiritual value, no contributions to the kingdom of God. It will all perish with the rest of the world and its material goods. It means nothing!" In 70 A.D., the temple was razed to the ground under the siege of Titus. The temple was burned along with more than 6,000 Jews, and no temple has ever been rebuilt.

You see, the most valuable gifts we can give are those that help people in need, not in building magnificent structures "for God." God has no need for such things! You may recall that even Jesus preached on the hillsides! He fed the five thousand in the open fields and hillside. The great revivalists in Church history, men like Geoge Whitefield, John Wesley, Dwight L. Moody, among others, had their greatest successes in the open fields!

Buildings don't save souls. Unless we build houses for people to live in, what good is a beautiful sanctuary? If we don't feed starving people and witness to them about the compassion of our Lord Jesus Christ, what good are padded pews and gold-plated offering trays?

Let me remind you of what Jesus told the religious people who did so much in His name in Matthew 25:44–46: "Then shall they also answer him, saying, Lord, when saw we thee an hungred, or athirst, or a stranger, or naked, or sick, or in prison, and did not minister unto thee? Then shall he answer them, saying, Verily I say unto you, Inasmuch as ye did it not to one of the the least of these, ye did it not to me. And these shall go away into everlasting punishment: but the righteous into life eternal."

When Jesus died on the cross, the only possession He had for the Romans to gamble over was the robe that they had ruthlessly torn from His body. You might ask, "But what did Jesus give or invest?" Obviously, He gave the greatest gift of all. He gave Himself, and that is worth more than all of the material wealth in all of God's creation!

Pulling the Lever

***For they that are after the flesh do mind the things of the flesh; but they that are after the Spirit the things of the Spirit.* [Romans 8:5]**

I watched one "prosperity" preacher tell his audience, "Money is supposed to come to you. Turn to somebody and say 'I'm supposed to be rich.' Turn to somebody else and say, 'I'm supposed to be wealthy.'" And like robots the crowd repeated his words and gestures.

He continued, "Everybody look at me and say, 'Money cometh to me *now*!' It won't come unless we put a *demand* on it." Then he had the crowd stand and go through the motions of pulling invisible slot machine levers while chanting, "Moneeeeeeey cometh to me—*now*!" He repeated his ritual several times, then said, "You're putting the *demand* up to *God*!" I had to grit my teeth. How dare anyone demand anything from Almighty God!

The claim that God *owes* us money—or anything else—is utter nonsense. More than that, it is outright blasphemy, and anyone who buys into it is just as wicked as the purveyors of greed theology. It is of the devil, and those who do these things are some of those to whom Jesus will say, "Depart from me ye workers of iniquity. I never knew you," when they face the judgment at the end of the age.

Remember, if it isn't in the Bible, it is just a gimmick used by those who would grab your money and run. They are charlatans from the word *go*.

This brings us to a point that needs to be addressed because more and more of these false prophets are misusing the Scriptures or creating their own versions or, for that matter, quoting from any one of the plethora of so-called new translations. It is a major problem in today's churches when we rely on a preacher to accurately and seriously divide the Word of God. When anyone stands in the pulpit and declares that "the Bible says," you have to know which Bible he is referring to—if, indeed, he is quoting any Bible at all.

It is important to recognize the swelling production of Bible versions today for what it really is. Satan has found a deceptive and diabolical way of bringing mass confusion to the churches of the last days. Should you question whether or not the devil is at the bottom of this diversionary tactic, Paul said in 1 Corinthians 14:33, "For God is not the author of confusion, but of peace, as in all churches of the saints."

The latest "translations" are no more than "paraphrased" Bibles—constituting nothing but commentaries on what the "translators" *think* God probably meant to say but just didn't know how to say it so that we could really understand it. Worse yet, they "translate" into what they *want* the Bible to say!

When I worked for Moody Press, Ken Taylor, the writer of *The Living Bible*, told me that he had never meant for the book to be published as a Bible, but rather as he originally intended it to be—a paraphrasing in his own words of the *Authorized Version* [KJV] so that his own children could better understand it. He titled his works *Living Letters* before expanding it to include the Gospels, and later, the Old Testament. Evidently, after Billy Graham offered it to his listeners, the book's popularity took off, and the publisher decided to re-introduce it as *the Living Bible. It is not the Word of God,* but rather the words of Ken Taylor as he wanted his own children to see it. This is not a criticism of Mr. Taylor or his work, for whom I have a high regard, but simply an explanation for his writing the book.

The vast majority of so-called Bible translations do not reflect the Hebrew and Greek accurately enough to be called the Word of God. Therefore, they constitute nothing more than forgeries of the Word! As of this date, the most accurate word-for-word translation of the Bible in English is still the *Authorized* or *King James Version* of the Bible.

I preached at a church where a very dear friend was a member. She took exception to a word for which I had given a literal Greek rendering. "My Bible doesn't say that!" she loudly proclaimed.

When she told me which version she was using, I had to explain, "That's because *your* Bible isn't *the* Bible, but rather a man's opinion of what the Bible says. In other words, it is little more than a Bible commentary."

Of course, that didn't make her any happier, but then, she once asked me, knowing that I have two graduate degrees in a field of psychology, "How can you reconcile the Bible with what you've learned from psychology?"

Once again I failed to make her happy. I simply told her that I would never think of reconciling the Bible—God's Word—with man's vain attempts to undermine God's Word with confused psychological theories. Romans 3:4 exhorts us to "let God be true, but every man a liar."

My wife and I find it frustrating when we can't follow the Bible references in the preachers' sermons since they seemingly never use the same version twice! Make no mistake, they are not *all* His Word since none of them say the same things. Most of them are published in an effort to teach a particular theology that may or may not be what the original Scriptures taught—but they do succeed in tickling the ears of those who use them and stuffing the pockets of those who wrote them. You see, when we permit this kind of deception, it opens the door to believing whatever we want to believe. If you don't like what one version has to say, then you can always find a version that will be more to your liking. If you choose to believe something the Scriptures don't teach, then you can simply create your own scriptures, using God's Word as a general guideline, and call them a Bible quotation.

In her editorial in the December 6, 2006 edition of *The Wall Street Journal* titled *Heavens, Bibles Are Really Booming*, Joanne Kaufman quoted Rodney Hatfield of Bible publisher Thomas Nelson, Inc., who said, "But now pastors are reaching out and grabbing the translation that best suits their point for a particular sermon." Such preachers don't care whether they are using an accurate translation or not as long as it says what they *want* it to say!

When you listen to anyone who starts by saying, "The Bible says," you need to have your Bible in hand in order to verify that the speaker is really stating what appears in the scriptures. I have discovered that today's false prophets use the term to mean "in my opinion," giving his or her opinion as though it were indeed the Word of God.

It becomes an expression of opinion by the interpreter in order to lead the listener away from the firm foundation God has given us in His Word and into the "damnable heresy" that the Apostle Peter warns about in 2 Peter 2:1: "There shall be false teachers among you, who privily shall bring in damnable heresies, even denying the Lord that bought them and bring upon themselves swift destruction. And many shall follow their pernicious ways; by reason of whom the way of truth shall be evil spoken of. And through *covetousness* [belying their greed theology] shall they with feigned [*fabricated*] words make merchandise of you [by taking your money under false pretenses]: whose judgment now of a long time lingereth not, and their damnation slumbereth not."

Giving by Grace:

***I do not frustrate the grace of God: for if righteousness come by the law, then Christ is dead in vain.* [Galatians 2:21]**

There is a strange phenomenon among preachers in local churches that amazes me. We are told in no uncertain terms that salvation is received by grace through faith, "and that not of yourselves: it is the gift of God: Not of works, lest any man should boast" (Ephesians 2:8–9). That is, after all, what the Bible says. And regarding the law, Galatians 5:1 tells us to "stand fast therefore in the liberty wherewith Christ hath made us free, and be not entangled again with the yoke of bondage."

But, using circumcision as an example of the Old Testament law, Paul goes on to say, "For I testify again to every man that is circumcised, that he is a debtor to do the whole law. Christ is become of no effect unto you, whosoever of you are justified by the law; ye are *fallen from grace*. For we through the Spirit wait for the hope of righteousness *by faith*" (Galatians 5:3–5). In other words, if we place ourselves under one part of the law, we must also keep the rest of the law. In so doing, we become disclaimers of the efficacy of the work of Christ on the cross. We have placed ourselves back under the curse of the law. We are not true believers!

According to many otherwise fundamental preachers, that truth is only good so long as it does not affect their income or the income of the local church. Let me say up front that the local church is the foundation of today's worldwide outreach of the gospel and the communion of God's family. Today's church needs require the generous support of its members. But the particular preachers that I refer to are willing to make exceptions to God's holy Word—proving that money, or what the Bible calls "filthy lucre," is always a stumbling block to the spiritual vitality of many believers.

Giving to the ministry of the local church is an issue revolving around the Christian's use of money that causes much confusion and much contention—which, of course, should never happen. I have heard a great deal of preaching on this subject that was either sadly mistaken or deliberately deceptive. There will be those who may not appreciate what is covered in this section, but what I have to say is based squarely on the Word of God, not on the doctrines and creeds of any denomination, church, or preacher.

The error of greed theology not withstanding, when Christians give to the service of the Lord, they will be blessed in return—but not for the purpose of making them wealthy. Of course, their greatest reward is in Heaven, but I don't believe the Lord will allow those who give through the righteous intent of the heart to do without. As David said in Psalm 37:25, "I have been young, and now am old; yet have I not seen the righteous forsaken, nor his seed begging bread." Just because our treasure is laid up in Heaven does not mean that God forgets the needs of His people on Earth. He will meet our *needs*, but as I said in the previous section, there is no promise for our *wants*. As Paul reminds us in Philippians 4:19, "But my God shall supply all your *need* according to his riches in glory by Christ Jesus."

The problem we face in today's churches is that many of those who stand in our pulpits simply don't know how to encourage people to support the work of the local church and the worldwide community. As a result they inadvertently apply the Robb Thompson approach to giving—that "money is the vehicle through which God performs His will." They forget who is in control! God reminds us that He possesses all things in Psalm 50:10–12: "For every beast of the forest is mine, and the cattle upon a thousand hills. I know all the fowls of the mountains: and the wild beasts of the field are mine. If I were hungry, I would not tell thee: for the world is mine, and the fulness thereof." Our Lord will never run out of the provisions we need to accomplish His will! The church that is committed to Him will never have to worry about His provisions as long as its use of money is not abused.

As Jeanette and I have traveled around from church to church in our ministry, we have found that the smaller churches have been by far the most generous with their giving—especially the small country churches. They were not so constrained by the shackles of the worldly trappings that so many of our larger urban churches tie themselves to. They don't need fancy carpets, padded pews, gold-trimmed offering plates, expensive air-conditioning, equipment to project the preacher's face from the wall behind him or to provide the words to songs the congregation doesn't know because the church no longer uses the hymnal, or the finest P.A. systems they can find.

You might think that you can't "have church" without those things, but I would remind you that the great Metropolitan Tabernacle where Charles Hadden Spurgeon preached so eloquently to five thousand people at a time had none of those things. The church didn't even have electricity. The same things were true of George Whitefield, John Wesley, Dwight L. Moody, and virtually all those who experienced the great revivals throughout the history of the Church. Frankly, we have been so spoiled by our modern conveniences and comforts that we can't comprehend doing without them. We think we need them, but the day may come soon when the Lord will take them away.

My wife spent years in the rain forest of the Congo living in a mud house with her parents. They held services in a church that was made of mud with a grass roof. There was no glass in the windows, no electricity, no piano, no organ, and none of the trappings of an American church. Yet, they had everything they needed to worship together—and delighted in doing so!

The churches of the twenty-first century certainly don't function the same way the Church did in the apostolic years of the New Testament. Since the early Church didn't meet in church buildings, giving was used primarily to feed the poor. For the first three hundred years after Pentecost, churches did not receive tithes but did receive free-will offerings for the needy.

But let's face it, until recent years, the local churches were a mainstay for supporting missionaries and evangelists, as well as helping the poor. Now those local churches have become a home away from home with all the comforts the world has to offer. They can no longer afford to support God's worldwide ministry of spreading the gospel. While they wallow in their wealth they have become a spiritual blight on the historic Church of Jesus Christ!

Now the economy has plunged, and giving in the local churches has decreased. How will they ever pay for the extravagances of their buildings and the modern comforts to which they have become addicted?

We know that the real Church consists of *people*, not *buildings*. But when we talk about the church today, we usually think of the building in which people meet to worship. Many of these buildings are meeting places for unregenerate, though perhaps religious, folk who either have a vested interest in the "organization" or who think somehow their faithfulness to the church will enhance their chances in eternity. Church buildings cost money, much more today than they did decades ago—and most certainly in many cases far more costly than necessary for the gathering of the saints. The utility bills need to be paid. The pastors and salaried staff require their paychecks. The money must come from someplace.

In order to meet the financial needs of the modern church's programs and property, there must be a system for raising the necessary funds. Most churches insist that this must be done by the giving of tithes and free-will offerings. Unlike the Old Testament tithe of crops and wine to the priests and Levites for food, sacrifices, and feeding the poor, the tithe today is considered by these churches to be a tenth of one's earnings, and the insistence upon this as a minimum of the member's giving has brought debates about its meaning or even its validity. Forget the fact that tithing is a part of the Old Testament law. It's the only way church leaders can think of to encourage their members to pay their dues!

I have heard people argue about whether it must be a tenth of one's gross earnings or net earnings. After all, the government takes a large portion of your wages long before you ever get paid. The argument can be made that this portion was never yours. It was the government's. You never touched nor had the opportunity to use it. Then some have wondered whether it comes before or after the necessary bills are paid—rent or house payment, utilities, food, and so forth. In other words, people often try to find ways of skirting the tithe or limiting their personal costs for attending church.

Of course, all of these points of contention amount to exactly what the Pharisees would have argued. The problem is that these folk have the proverbial cart before the horse. Our churches have adopted the position that our government has taken—spend, spend, spend. "Never mind our ability to pay. We'll find a way to get the money." I have yet to attend a church whose monthly budget doesn't fall short of its requirements.

We conducted evangelistic meetings in a church in a small mountain community where there was a major division over the pastor's decision to build a $100,000 gymnasium. At that time it was a lot of money. It still is, but not close to what it would cost today. The pastor wanted me to use my ministry to help persuade the congregation to get behind him. Oddly enough, another member of the church asked me to persuade the pastor not to spend the money on such a project because the church was falling short of its budget every month.

I told them both that God called me to preach the gospel, not to raise funds for building gymnasiums. Besides, I wouldn't have been much help because I was convinced that such a project for that church in that particular community would be a misuse of the Lord's money. Why? Because the community already had a public gymnasium and because the Lord did not call us to build gymnasiums but to preach the gospel. Do we really want our children to think they serve the Lord by bouncing rubber balls around on a gym floor? Mind you, this church didn't have a Christian school that would require physical education.

One could argue that a gymnasium could be used to bring Christian young people together and provide them with wholesome activities. That may be true, but I could have done it on a lot less than $100,000! Just think of how many poor people could have been fed with that money. Is it more important to play games or feed poor people? How many missionaries could be provided for with that money? Would a shelter for homeless people be more important than a gymnasium for pampered teenagers? Would a supply of medicine or books or Bibles for needy people here or overseas be a better investment?

Remember Matthew 25:34–36: "Then shall the King say unto them on his right hand, Come, ye blessed of my Father, inherit the kingdom prepared for you from the foundation of the world: For I was an hungred, and ye gave me meat: I was thirsty, and ye gave me drink: I was a stranger, and ye took me in: Naked, and ye clothed me: I was sick, and ye visited me: I was in prison, and ye came unto me."

Then the righteous will ask the King when it was that they had done these things, and He will respond, "Inasmuch as ye have done it unto one of the least of these my brethren, ye have done it unto me" (verse 40). It is interesting that the Lord did not say, "And you provided me with a place to play games."

With these Scriptures in mind, what do you think is the greatest investment in the Lord's work: money or good works? While there is no question that today's churches need money in order to conduct their affairs, nonetheless, it seems appropriate to ask whether the Lord emphasizes giving a tenth of *His* money to the local church or helping people who are in need.

You see, under the law of Christ, *everything* you have or earn belongs to Him. One hundred percent—not just ten percent! Never forget that Jesus is the Lord of all those who call upon Him. He is the Lord of the Church and of every individual believer. *Nothing* belongs to you. It *all* belongs to Him, and you are responsible for making sure His belongings are used wisely for His glory.

If you are going to "give to the Lord," you can't very well throw your money into the air and say, "Here, catch!" How do you give to the Lord? By helping other people! That may require money, but more often it requires *you.*

When I was very young, my mother developed rheumatic fever. She was bedfast for a long time, and as she slowly regained her health, she was held back by her physical weakness and pain. A neighbor whom we knew nothing about came to our house every day to help Mom with the housekeeping. It was unusual because we lived in a close-knit neighborhood and thought we knew everyone. She made sure the children were cared for and kept the house clean. To this day I don't even know her name, but *God does*! Perhaps she was one of those "angels unaware" that the writer of Hebrews spoke about (Hebrews 13:2). She did those things "unto the least of these my brethren." She didn't throw a ten dollar bill at

Mom and say, "I hope you get better." Instead, day after day, week after week, until my mother was well, she gave of *herself.*

I hear continually that people just don't have the time to spend with other people. They don't have time to attend revivals or evangelistic meetings. They don't have time to visit unsaved folk or housebound believers in need of comfort and fellowship. "After all," they say, "it takes two people to make a living these days, and when we get home from work, we just want to relax."

"Horse feathers!" my dad would have said. That's what I call a "cop out." The reason it takes two to earn a living is because Americans are used to living high on the proverbial hog. We like to have things—certainly far more than we need. We all need to visit a Third World country and see the way the common people live. My wife lived in a mud hut in the African rain forest for four years. Her family had no running water, no indoor toilet, no access to a grocery store or clothing store or even a gas station. Their books and papers mildewed. Even my wife's accordion, which she used for her ministry, mildewed. They had no paved roads, and the roads they had were only one-way. If you met an oncoming vehicle, you had to back up, perhaps for a mile or more. The roads often consisted of two ruts in the mud. It almost cost the lady who was to become my wife her life when she had an attack of appendicitis, and she had to help push their vehicle out of the mud on the way to the hospital many miles away.

In spite of the fact that both husband and wife work outside the home and are tired when they get home, the excuse is still without merit. During the great American revivals and brush arbor meetings in the early 1800s, men worked from sun-up to sun-down at hard labor, usually on a farm following a mule-pulled plow. At the same time the women gathered from the fields and prepared food for hours over a hot stove or oven without electricity or gas, which meant they had to also continually replace the wood for fire—among a myriad of other chores inside and outside. They were eager to help those in need, those who were sick or suffering some other hardship—all of that and children and home to care for! They had a sense of community. Today, most Americans don't even know their neighbors' names.

We think we have accomplished a great service for the Lord if we get up the gumption to attend church on Sunday morning, to put a few dollars in the offering plate to maintain the facilities, or even sing in the choir.

As long as we are going to grace the church with our presence, we might as well do it in the most comfortable environment. Many, if not most, modern church buildings are constructed for their aesthetic properties, their grandeur, their comfort, their pomp—in other words, how pleasant they are to look at and how comfortable they make us feel. In fact, they provide more comfort for us a few hours each week than the average family around the world experiences in a life-time.

Very few churches are built with simplicity and austerity. I once attended a seminar on the psychology of church building and expansion. The leader went to great lengths to explain how color combinations (pastel versus bright or bold), padding for the pews, tones and quality of the carpets, position of the pulpit, and the best use of a carillon, among other things, would affect the emotions and attention of the people in the congregation. I felt sick to my stomach!

We put more emphasis and spend more money on the building we worship in than we do the worship we participate in! In fact, most of those who attend church services don't even know what it means to worship. Stained-glass windows don't teach us the Word of God or win people to Jesus Christ. They don't bring us any closer together as the family of God. They are beautiful to look at, but that is only a characteristic of what the Bible calls *vanity*. We take pride in the things we can buy and build. When pride enters the picture, it becomes a dangerous situation— especially for the church. Never forget that "pride goeth before destruction, and an haughty spirit before a fall" (Proverbs 16:18). Perhaps that is why so many churches and denominations have fallen away from the fundamentals of the faith, and many have closed their doors.

I've seen a television program that is shown every week and greatly admire the preacher. He preaches God's Word and refuses to compromise what he believes to be true to the Bible. However, his cameras tend to accentuate the grandeur of his church facilities—especially the magnificent display of pipes for the pipe organ and the beautiful decor. His is an example of the conflict between worldly vanity and spiritual preaching—between the preaching of the Word and the shameful application his church makes of it.

I once served as interim pastor at a small country church that had been a German Presbyterian Church before becoming an independent community church. There was an antique sign above the door written in German, and the building had no cross above it. Two of the older women of the church fought tooth-and-nail to keep the sign because it reminded them of the old days when their grandparents had helped found the church. There were also two smelly outhouses behind the building. The older ladies thought this contributed to the "rustic appearance" or "atmosphere" of the church, but I knew that the only atmosphere they contributed to was the stink, as well as the contamination of the nearby well. The health department had condemned the well, but the women continued to drink from the pump.

Even worse, a group of teenagers from a neighboring town had seen the strange words on the German sign above the door and concocted a story of how the facility was a place where devil-worshipers held their occult meetings. Not only did they use this as an excuse to vandalize the property, but the church had always provided them with outdoor facilities for relieving their beer-filled bladders. As a result, every Saturday night the building was vandalized with fire-bombs, blood, broken windows, and uprooted pews. The local authorities did nothing to help, so the members took turns sitting in front of the church building every Saturday night to protect it, then slept through most of the Sunday service—all because of the vanity of a couple of influential members.

I had suggested building indoor facilities, but the ladies blew their proverbial corks. Out of desperation, an elder and I decided to conduct a night attack against the outhouses, plowing them to the ground and burying the remnants. The next week we introduced the members to our new indoor restrooms.

Regardless of the fact that the early Church was

not concerned with the kinds of expenses our modern churches incur, these expenses are here to stay. We will continue to assemble ourselves together, share the good fellowship of God's children, listen to the preacher as he attempts to rightly divide the Word *for* us, pray together, and experience all of the "add-ons" that were never considered by the early Church.

What the church expects in return is that we pay for the privilege of using its facilities and the talents of its ministers. Believe me, it takes a lot of money to build and maintain the church facilities and to pay the salaries of all of the ministers and employees required for today's urban churches. The problem arises in the methods used to raise the money. This brings us back to that nagging and divisive issue. In most churches, those in charge tell us about that Old Testament law that we are still required to obey—the law of *tithing*.

In Malachi 3:6, God tells His people, "For I am the Lord, I change not." Though God never changes, the way in which He deals with His people does. The Old Testament explains the way God dealt with Israel, the channel through which He brought His only begotten Son into the world. The New Testament deals with a new generation of believers called the Church, a chosen people who are not supposed to operate under the curse of the Old Testament law of Moses but under the New Testament law of liberty—the law of Christ.

I heard a preacher tell his congregation, "You'd pay a high price to go to a football game, especially the Super Bowl. You'd pay a good price for seats at the Municipal Opera in St. Louis, but when it comes to giving to the Lord, some of you hold back." Perhaps that's because they don't think the church is supposed to be viewed the same way. In other words, their hedonistic appetites are more important to them than God's work! I would far rather see Christian people forego wasting their money on those worldly amusements and use the money for serving the Lord—including meeting the needs of the local church.

For most people, what the preacher said is probably true. At the same time, many churches today treat the gospel like a game or sports competition. I lived in a town that had fourteen churches of the same denomination with "bus ministries." Their buses routinely passed each other, criss-crossing the community to see how many members or children they could steal from their "competitors"—their "sister" churches. It was more of a numbers game than a tool for winning youngsters to the Lord or giving them sound Bible teaching. They could boast that they had umpteen children in Sunday School that week. I heard one youngster brag about joining several different churches and getting baptized in each one simply because he would be picked up by various church buses who would bribe him with food or other gifts to attend their Sunday Schools.

People attend church services for a variety of reasons. For one, they are taught that it is a *sin* not to go to church. After all, Hebrews 10:24–25 exhorts us: "And let us consider one another to provoke unto love and to good works: Not forsaking the assembling of ourselves together, as the manner of some is; but exhorting one another: and so much the more, as ye see the day approaching."

The strange thing about it is that they usually only get

the "not forsaking the assembling of ourselves together" part and almost never hear the "provoke unto love and good works," which includes the only part of the passage that *is* a commandment.

There is no sin involved in not attending a particular church. There were no church buildings when that passage was written. The believers in the early Church met in their own homes. There was still a Jewish temple and many synagogues, but the gospel was not welcome there. Acts 2:46 says, "And they, continuing daily with one accord in the temple, and breaking bread from house to house, did eat their meat with gladness and singleness of heart." The first Christians were Jews who were accustomed to meeting at the temple, but as the Church grew and the gospel prospered, Christians were denied access to the temple.

Acts 20:20 tells how Paul taught from house to house, and in Romans 16:3–5, Paul directed the recipient of his letter to "Greet Priscilla and Aquila my helpers in Christ Jesus . . . Likewise greet the church that is in their house." From that point, he salutes the churches that represent five different households of various believers. That is perfectly in keeping with what Jesus taught in Matthew 18:20, "For where two or three are gathered together in my name, there am I in the midst of them." That means that the Church is wherever those two or three believers are.

We must realize that, in the early church, there was no Baptist Church, Presbyterian Church, Methodist Church, Assembly of God, and so forth. There was only one Church, and it was called *the Church of God*. The Church of God was called in its various geographical locations the Church at Ephesus, the Church at Jerusalem (which quickly had grown to many thousands), or the Church at Corinth, for example. There were no buildings for those arms of the Church to meet in, so they met from house to house in small groups.

Social pressure is another reason people attend church. I always cringe at election time when candidates show up in the front pews of our churches or when folks attend church on Easter or Christmas so their children can get free goodies.

I listened to students joking about watching the ladies' bonnets flying down the windy streets of Chicago when I served at Moody Church in 1963. Most of them were lifted from heads that only darkened the church doors in their Easter finery on Easter Sunday.

By and large, however, most people attend church because they want to be taught from the Word of God, to share the fellowship of other believers, to worship together, "singing and making melody in their hearts to the Lord," and to have the assurance that there are others who care about them. These are people who look for ways that they can serve the Lord and often need the assistance of someone who has the spiritual gifts to show them how. They don't attend to be entertained. They are there to give of themselves, to worship the Lord together, to edify one another, and to receive spiritual blessings from the Lord. So there is no reason to buy a ticket for admission. It is not a ball game or a concert performance or a stage production (or at least, shouldn't be). It is *worship* and *fellowship in the Spirit*, and if it isn't, then it isn't church. There is no price for worship. Giving must come from the heart and the ability to give—but above all, it isn't *law*.

One might ask, "But what about Malachi 3:8? Doesn't that establish the law of tithing?"

My answer would be, "Absolutely!"—*if* it is kept in the context in which it was given. But many preachers who have to protect their paychecks and the expenses of their platform are not willing to do that. Malachi 3:7–8 says: "Even from the days of your fathers ye are gone away from mine ordinances [the Levitical law], and have not kept them. Return unto me, and I will return unto you, saith the Lord of hosts. But ye said, Wherein shall we return? [Notice the preceding verse is *never* cited from today's pulpits when verse 8 is used.] Will a man rob God? Yet ye have robbed me. But ye say, Wherein have we robbed thee? In tithes and offerings."

The temple was the ruling force in Israel, and the priests and Levites received their food from the tithes. It included tithing their crops, livestock, and wine. It was used to feed the priests, as well as to feed the poor.

The reference to God's ordinances in verse 7 was to the Levitical law and included much more than the tithes and offerings. These were examples the Lord used to show Israel how it had turned away from God's authority. One could say that the pocketbook contained the spirituality of Israel. Their failure to obey this part of the law was a symptom of the greater sin. That is why verse 9 says, "Ye are cursed with a curse: for ye have robbed me, even this whole nation." By refusing to support the temple, which represented the very presence of God in the world, they were denying His authority over the entire nation.

In addition to neglecting the temple, verse 13 says that they spoke against God: "Your words have been stout against me, saith the Lord. Yet ye say, What have we spoken so much against thee?" The word "stout" implies the kind of animosity toward God that the Jews had against Stephen when they "gnashed on him with their teeth."

Verse 14 explains, "Ye have said, It is vain to serve God: and what profit is it that we have kept his ordinance, and that we have walked mournfully before the Lord of hosts?"

You see, the curse was not about tithes and offerings; it was about Israel's turning away from God. They accused God of ignoring their needs, of taking from them and not blessing them in return. That is why the tithe was used as an example of their disobedience.

But what has all that to do with the Church of Jesus Christ? Nothing! It has to do only with Israel as the nation applied the Law in obedience to God. The Law is a curse, and those who are under the Law are still under a curse. They are not true believers!

Let me make the issue clear. There is no reference at all in the New Testament to a law of tithing regarding the Church, nor is there any reference to individual believers where tithing is concerned. It seems that there are some people who for want of a specific doctrine in the Bible choose to create their own Scriptures or doctrines in order to force their opinions on others— claiming, of course, that they are Biblical truths. These preachers are no different from the Pharisees who created their own rules for the Jews to follow.

When our government spends too much money, the politicians have found two ways to make up for their incompetent behavior. They increase taxes or simply print more money. Either way, the taxpayers have been ripped off, and our economy has crumbled.

A church cannot afford to spend more than it takes in. If it can't meet its budget, then the budget should be reduced. If the church can't pay for it, the church doesn't need it!

Where those who spend the church's money are concerned, they can neither increase taxes nor print more money. They are far more creative than that. They either make new laws, or they reach back into the Old Testament to find a law they can enforce. They become modern-day judaizers and convince their members that they are still under a particular part of the law. They are the same kind of people that caused Paul to write his epistle to the Galatians—legalists who would rob believers of their freedom, turning the grace of God into a curse.

However, there is a legitimate principle that could be applied to the Church. If the local church is the center of our worship and outreach, then we need to give that congregation our support, whether with money, goods, spiritual gifts, or talents, without which the church cannot thrive. But by no means must we ever tell a believer that he is robbing God if he is generously following what he understands the New Testament to teach.

At the same time, those who hold positions in the ministry of the local church should not be greedy. I know of a church where the pastor received a salary five times that of the average family income in that congregation while using the pulpit to accuse the people of "robbing God" because not everyone tithed! He was more concerned about *his* wealth than the needs of the people who paid his salary. Hence, he became another modern-day judaizer.

There is no evidence in the New Testament that *any* of God's servants received regular wages from the Church. We do know that the Apostle Paul occasionally resorted to making tents to bring in some income and that the church at Philippi sent him some sort of gift to help him along while he was in prison, but Paul said that no other church communicated with him about finances (Philippians 4:15). We also know that some of the apostles continued to fish and that Paul's fellow-traveler, Luke, was a physician.

I attended a church that had formed a search committee to locate a potential pastoral candidate. They were shocked at the financial demands that were made by newly graduated Bible college or seminary students—as much as $100,000 per year. The church would have been hard pressed to pay $40,000. Greed has consumed the ministry in America!

The fact is that the Bible exhorts those who would be leaders in the churches to accomplish their service as examples to others and to do it without a concern for receiving payment in this world's goods. The Apostle Peter exhorts in 1 Peter 5:2–3: "Feed the flock of God which is among you, taking the oversight thereof, not by constraint [*not because you have to*], but willingly [*but because you want to*]; not for filthy lucre [*greed* or *financial gain*], but of a ready mind; Neither as being lords over God's heritage, but being ensamples to the flock."

The problem we face in today's churches is that we are trying to apply Old Testament structure under the curse of the law of Moses to New Testament grace under the law of Christ, and it doesn't work. In Galatians 3:24–25 Paul said, "Wherefore the law was our schoolmaster to bring us unto Christ, that we might be justified by faith. But after faith is come, we are no longer under a schoolmaster."

The word *tithe* only appears four times in the entire New Testament, and it is *only* used in the context of something that happened in, or relates to, the Old Testament. Matthew 23:23 and Luke 11:42, relate the same event, where Jesus is castigating the Pharisees. "Woe unto you, scribes and Pharisees, hypocrites! For ye pay tithe of mint and anise and cummin, and have omitted the weightier matters of *the law*, judgment, mercy, and faith: these ought ye to have done, and not to leave the other undone."

Notice that no money was mentioned. Can you see the reaction of a church pastor if you paid him in mint, anise or cummin? But it doesn't really matter. Jesus is speaking to Jews, the leaders of the Jews, who were under the curse of the law. He was talking about their hypocrisy in making a show of tithing and ignoring the more important elements of the law—judgment, mercy, and faith. These, by the way, are the same elements that have their roots within the framework of the law of Christ, the law of love.

In Luke 18:10–14, once again a Pharisee, *a hypocrite*, boasts about his piety in his prayers. In this text, Jesus said: "Two men went up into *the temple* to pray; the one a Pharisee, and the other a publican. The Pharisee stood and prayed thus with himself, God, I thank thee, that I am not as other men are, extortioners, unjust, adulterers, or even as this publican. I fast twice in the week, I give tithes of all that I possess. And the publican, standing afar off, would not lift up so much as his eyes unto heaven, but smote upon his breast, saying, God be merciful to me a sinner. I tell you, this man went down to his house justified rather than the other: for every one that exalteth himself shall be abased; and he that humbleth himself shall be exalted."

Not much on which to build a case for tithing, is it? Remember, our Lord was talking about Jews who were under the curse of the law of Moses.

The book of Hebrews relates the account of Abraham paying tithes to Melchisedec, the Prince of Peace. In its context, it has nothing to do with money, but with *homage*. Melchisedec was described in every way as the person of Jesus Christ. He was the Prince or King of Peace, who had no father or mother or descent. He had no beginning or ending, "but [was] made like unto the Son of God" (Hebrews 7:3). Abraham used the tithe to show that he gave greater honor to this eternal priest than to any earthly power. Abraham did not tithe to the Lord because he *had to* but because he *wanted* to, and he did not tithe from his own property, but from the spoils of war! Neither did he tithe money, but of whatever he was able to take from his enemies (Hebrews 7:4).

Regarding the issue of tithing, Hebrews 7:11–18 tells us that the law of tithing was *annulled* by the Lord Jesus Christ. Verses 15–16 puts it this way: "And it is yet far more evident: for that after the similitude of Melchisedec there ariseth another priest, Who is made, *not after the law of a carnal commandment*, but after the power of an endless life."

Verse 18 makes it as clear as day: "For there is verily a *disannulling* [literally, *cancellation*] *of the commandment* [including the law of tithing] going before for the weakness and unprofitableness thereof. For the law made nothing perfect, but the bringing in of a better hope did; by the which we draw nigh unto God."

Up to this point the seventh chapter of Hebrews is focused entirely on what was practiced in Israel under the Old Covenant—specifically where Abraham paid tithes to Melchisedec. Oddly enough, the Levitical law, including that of tithing, had not yet been given. Hence, Abraham tithed directly to the King of Peace of his own free will without the law! At the same time, his offering was a prevenient gift looking forward to the Levitical priesthood that was to spring from Abraham's seed. However, when *the commandment* is referred to in verse 18, the focus is on the Levitical law of tithing, though it may also extend to the rest of the Law.

Knowing this, it is obvious that if any informed preacher who has otherwise rightly divided the Word tells us that *tithing* is a commandment for Christian believers, he has either closed his mind to the truth or has been deluded by church tradition. Others abuse the Word of God to satisfy their own lust for money. Of course, there are still those preachers who preach through naiveté or ignorance because they fail to "rightly divide the Word."

The Law did not exist at the time of Abraham; neither did the temple; there was no ordinance, no commandment for tithing. The temple was temporal, as was the Law, but Christ is eternal. The Law was a curse, and the temple was man's way of approaching God and receiving forgiveness for sins. Jesus *is* God, who alone has the power to forgive sins and whose law is the law of perfect love!

Christians who are members of a local church and desire to see that church thrive should unquestionably support that church with whatever they are capable of giving, whether it be money, or material goods, or talents and spiritual gifts, but there is no *law* that requires anyone to pay tithes. God enables us to earn money so that we can use it for His glory, but when it comes to giving to the Lord, there is some confusion brought on by the deliberate mismanagement of the Word of God from so many pulpits.

There are many ways of giving to the Lord, and establishing at least a tenth of the family's income is an excellent way of voluntarily giving to the church. It is the traditional way of giving to your local church, or to your denomination, or to their related missionary endeavors. Others give to television and radio ministries, Christian schools, and evangelists. I have been an evangelist for over forty years, and while I have worked at a number of jobs to support my family, there were still those who provided us with financial support as we traveled—not because we asked them to, for we certainly did not—but because they wanted to help us with the costs of traveling across the country in God's service. They were aware of the fact that we had given up all of our earthly possessions that weren't related to our ministry—no house to go home to.

As essential as these ministries may be, however, they are not the *primary* Biblical ways of giving to the Lord. In fact, some of these "ministries" may not be receiving and using your gifts for the Lord, but rather for their own selfish and greedy interests. I heard one popular television evangelist who had passionately pleaded with his viewers to help him raise two million dollars to aid the children of Costa Rica tell an interviewer that, while he did receive the money from his supporters, it didn't actually go to help those children. He said, "Why, they wouldn't know what to do with that kind of money." When asked what he had done with the money, he said that "to be frank and honest with you, I don't know." He explained that his organization did not keep accurate records of how they used the donations they received. Later, this preacher was caught on more than one occasion, using some of *the Lord's* money to have sexual escapades with prostitutes. That's what Jesus meant when He said, "And the cares of this world, and the deceitfulness of riches, and the lusts of other things entering in, choke the word, and it becometh unfruitful" (Mark 4:19).

Many electronic preachers, such as the one I just mentioned, live high on the proverbial hog, driving new Lincoln Continentals or Cadillacs, wearing expensive jewelry, owning fine luxury homes and tropical condominiums, flying their own jet airplanes, sporting very expensive suits and designer shoes, taking cruises around the world, and using your money for many other worldly purposes. Though they work in the name of Christ, the people who do these things are not Christians. So when you give your money to them, you are *not* giving to the Lord!

Mind you, that does not mean that it is necessarily a sin for a Christian to own any of these things, but it *is* a sin to take the sacrificial gifts of Christian people to live a life of luxury—and especially when people have been told that the money would be used for something else, something that would truly be a service for the Lord! By the way, this description is *typical* of those who preach *greed theology*!

Paul said in 2 Corinthians 11:13–14, "For such are false apostles [*teachers*], deceitful workers, transforming themselves into the apostles of Christ. And no marvel; for Satan himself is transformed into an angel of light."

How many unsaved people can you think of who would give their hearts to the Lord if their only knowledge of other Christians rested in these kinds of charlatans? Can you imagine the struggle a person would go through when being wooed by the Holy Spirit while at the same time being repelled by these ungodly wolves in sheep's clothing? Once again, that's what the Apostle Peter meant when he warned us to "be sober, be vigilant; because your adversary the devil, as a roaring lion, walketh about, seeking whom he may devour" (1 Peter 5:8). The men and women I have described are emissaries of Satan.

Christians are admonished by Peter in the next verse, "Whom resist stedfast in the faith, knowing that the same afflictions are accomplished in your brethren that are in the world."

What, then, are the primary *Biblical* ways of giving to the Lord? The first and most important use for a Christian's giving is found in Ephesians 4:28, "Let him that stole steal no more: but rather let him labour, working with his hands the thing which is good, that he may have *to give to him that needeth.*" Isn't it ironic that Paul tells the ex-thief that the primary reason for his earning wages is to give to those who need it?

The fact is, however, that the Christian's greatest outreach for giving to the Lord is to give to the poor or to a brother or sister who is in need—if a family loses its house to a fire, if a woman left alone by the death of her husband is in need, if a violent storm has taken the possessions of a neighbor, if someone is sick and in need of help—these and countless other needs may arise that require the aid of a Christian's resources. More money and material goods were given by Christian people to those who lost their homes in New Orleans and the surrounding area after Hurricane Katrina than ever before in history—so much so that Dr. D. James Kennedy had to issue a plea for funds to rebuild his work in Florida! He reported that gifts to his ministry had dropped so low that the church was caught off guard. He later reported that people gave the *millions* of dollars he needed in response to his plea. Perhaps those *millions* could have been used in better ways.

Proverbs 28:27 assures us, "He that giveth unto the poor shall not lack: but he that hideth his eyes shall have many a curse." There is both a promise and a warning in this verse. We are promised that our needs will be met when we share with needy people. We are also warned that if we turn our backs on those who are in need, we will be cursed. Perhaps we will someday find ourselves in their shoes.

When we were newlyweds, my wife and I moved to California so I could attend Biola College. We had gotten down to four dollars, and neither of us had been able to get a job. A young man and very dear friend, Frank Schultze, handed me fifty dollars after church. I found later that he had also given my wife fifty dollars. Then he told me not to leave because he wanted to have my car filled with gas. "This isn't a loan," he said. "Someday you will find someone else who is in a similar bind. I want you to help that person the same way." Then he slapped me on the back and walked away. I have since, on numerous occasions, followed Frank's advice, and every time I do, I remember my dear friend of long ago.

When John the Baptist was asked by the people, "What shall we do then? He answereth and saith unto them, He that hath two coats, let him impart to him that hath none; and he that hath meat, let him do likewise" (Luke 3:10–11).

In the same way, when Jesus spoke to the multitude on the Mount of Olives in Matthew 25:37–39, the righteous people had asked Him: "Lord, when saw we thee an hungred, and fed thee? Or thirsty, and gave thee drink? When saw we thee a stranger, and took thee in? Or naked, and clothed thee? Or when saw we thee sick, or in prison, and came unto thee?"

Our Lord's response was, "Verily I say unto you, Inasmuch as ye have done it unto one of the *least* of these my brethren, ye have done it unto me" (verse 40).

When Jesus spoke in the synagogue in Nazareth, He read from Isaiah, "The Spirit of the Lord is upon me, because he hath anointed me to preach the gospel to the poor; he hath sent me to heal the brokenhearted, to preach deliverance to the captives, and recovering of sight to the blind, to set at liberty them that are bruised, to preach the acceptable year of the Lord" (Luke 4:18–19). Then He added in verse 21, "This day is this scripture fulfilled in your ears." As His purchased possessions, we must follow His leadership. It is one way of giving to the Lord. Even though we may not always be in a position to go to such people, we can give to others so that they can go.

I'll never forget the experience I had as a teenager while riding through Chicago with my dad. We passed a row of eating places, and I noticed a ragged-looking man digging in a garbage dumpster. Then he pulled out some of its contents and began to eat it. "Ugh!" I said, "That man's eating garbage!"

"No, Son," my dad responded, "He's eating food that other people wasted. I suppose it's a good thing they wasted it, or he would have nothing to eat."

It's a shame that the Church of Jesus Christ is refusing to honor the Lord by failing to provide for the poor as Christ commanded. There are just too many frivolous things on which to spend "God's money."

Giving does not always require money or other material things. Sometimes we give of ourselves in praying with those who need prayer, in comforting those who need comforting, in giving the gospel when they need to be saved, but never forgetting that we can give a blanket to them when they are cold.

Does all of this mean that we are not to support the ministry of the local church? Of course not! But it does mean that we must be careful about the way we support the work of the Lord in or out of the local church and make sure that we care for the greatest needs first, in or out of the church—being careful not to waste it on frivolous or needless things. At the same time, Christians are instructed to care for the needs of their *brothers and sisters in Christ* above all else. "But whoso hath this world's good, and seeth his brother have need, and shutteth up his bowels of compassion from him, how dwelleth the love of God in him?" (1 John 3:17).

That verse is preceded immediately with "Hereby

perceive we the love of God, because he laid down his life for us: and we ought to lay down our lives for the brethren" (verse 16).

Verse 18, then, exhorts us, "My little children, let us not love in word, neither in tongue; but in *deed* and in truth."

This, then, is giving by grace.

Slain or Mesmerized?

***Let all things be done decently and in order.* [1 Corinthians 14:40]**

If you ever have reason to question the integrity of a religious doctrine or behavior, there is a simple solution. Look it up! If such a doctrine is not found in the Word of God, then it is not of God. It is of the devil. The apostles of greed have devised a number of their own rituals that are designed to please the flesh. They are hedonistic in nature. "If it feels good," they teach, "then do it!" That's where the emphasis is for those who preach the "gospel" of greed.

My wife, Jeanette, and I once attended a service in which the preacher made the mistake of saying that rejoicing is a way of showing our joy. Mind you, there was nothing wrong with what he said, but rather, where he said it and to whom he said it. "It brings a spirit of laughter to our hearts," he noted. A woman in the audience immediately began to laugh uncontrollably. In no time she was joined by other women until soon most of the women in the church were doubled over in a fit of spasmodic laughter. The pastor desperately tried to regain the attention of his audience to little avail. Finally, the laughter subsided, perhaps because the excitement wore off or their desire to clown around subsided. At that point, the young pastor attempted to cover the outrageous behavior by remarking that "this is either of the Lord, or we are a bunch of nuts!" Frankly, I would guess it was the latter. As I recall, without hesitation the minister quickly took an offering. After all, it was best to get it while the people were still in a mood for "rejoicing." From that time, as was reported to me, the services from week to week often rang out with fits of "laughing in the Spirit." I can't find any reference in the Scriptures to that spiritual gift!

The preachers of greed have misappropriated several Biblical truths and turned them into lies. They have also simply created their own set of behaviors to mislead people into situations that will bring more filthy lucre into their bank accounts and enable them to have greater control over their followers.

One such behavior is what they have slyly called being "slain in the Spirit." This irreverent idea is not even hinted at in the Bible, and one might question which "spirit" is slaying these folks. In this demonstration, a preacher pretends to have the gift of healing. In performing his show, he puts his hand on his victim's head and shoves her backward, sometimes so gently that she is not aware of it, and sometimes with an obvious "assist." She in turn falls into the waiting arms of the preacher's cohorts. Often before the woman falls backward, she begins to shake in an emotional seizure. This particular display is as far removed from the exhortation to "let all things be done decently and in order" as it can get. It is more illustrative of the kind of demonic activity that probably reigns in the Laodicean church, that is, the church of the last days described in Revelation 3:14–22.

This is the way it works: If you want to be healed or to have your miracle, you must rely on the preacher's instructions. You must be willing to humiliate yourself. Shake as though you are being jolted by electricity. Fall backward in a seeming faint and trust the preacher's colleagues to catch you before you break your neck on the stage floor.

These are the subtle techniques of brainwashing, which is only used for one purpose—to bring people under the manipulative control of the one who is programming their minds. In the case of the preacher of greed theology, it is to get control of their money, as well as their minds. The more followers the preacher can manipulate, the more wealth he or she will accumulate.

Benny Hinn, a popular Charismatic healer, routinely uses this ploy to create his miracles. Everyone who wants to be healed must, as part of the process, be slain in the Spirit. Hinn touches or pushes each one on the forehead and gestures for his subject to fall backward into the waiting arms of his catchers—who in turn lay the fallen victim on the floor, sometimes missing a direct catch at which time she will have a hard landing. Often, Hinn will simply wave his hand at his victims and give a prolonged serpentine *hiss* as he gestures for them to fall. The behavior appears to be much like a circus performance.

I watched one of Hinn's performances as one of his cohorts brought a crippled boy onto the stage. The assistant was waving a body and leg brace in the air and yelling that the boy had been healed of broken bones in his leg. The boy hobbled onto the stage, barely able to walk and in obvious pain. Hinn yelled words to the effect that "he has been completely healed, but the metal rods they put in his leg are causing him to walk like that. He is not really in pain!" Then he instructed the boy to go back to his doctor and have the metal pins removed from his leg.

In *every* case of healing in the Bible, the one being healed was instantly and completely healed. There was no need for gradually casting off the symptoms of their ailment. The blind man was given instant and complete sight (John 9). The lame man ran and leaped and praised God (Acts 3:8). The leper's hideous disease was *immediately* cleansed so that he could show his face without fear (Luke 5:13). In none of these cases did anyone hiss at them or cause them to fall backward under the spell of a healer.

I have completed graduate studies in a field of psychology in which I was taught that a counselor or therapist must always rely on the *feelings* of a client. The psychotherapist typically asks, "How do you feel about that?" Never, "What do you *think* about that?" The last thing a psychologist wants is for his client to think for himself. If the client continues to be reliant upon his feelings alone, then the therapist is able to maintain greater control over his client. That is exactly what happens between the greed preacher and his disciple. The preacher who is given to greed must have control or power over his follower or else he will not be able to control this individual's purse strings.

If we examine the events in the New Testament in which Jesus or His disciples healed anyone, we will not find a single example of being "slain in the Spirit." Surely, if a mere self-proclaimed healer of today can produce such a display, when the Lord of Glory healed anyone we would have seen a much greater display.

Let's take a closer look at that first apostolic miracle—the healing of the lame man at the temple gate—who gives the opposite reaction. The man sat at the gate as Peter and John approached him. When the lame man asked alms of the apostles, Peter said, "Silver and gold have I none; but such as I have give

I thee: In the name of Jesus Christ of Nazareth rise up and walk" (Acts 3:6).

As we read the text, the man did not fall backward in a faint, that is, being slain in the Spirit. Instead, "he [Peter] took him by the right hand, and lifted him up: and immediately his feet and ankle bones received strength. And he leaping up stood, and walked, and entered into the temple, walking, and leaping, and praising God" (7–8).

Instead of shaking and falling back in a faint, he leaped to his feet, walking, and leaping, and praising God! What a difference between the apostolic experience and today's fleshly exhibition! The one received his healing and rejoiced immediately, recognizing the glorious experience that came from Heaven, while the other reacts negatively, as though it were a painful ordeal. And guess what—Peter didn't asked for money!

The fact is that the only example of anyone falling down under the power of the Holy Spirit, apart from Saul of Tarsus, was that of Ananias and Sapphira who lied to the Holy Spirit about what they had given to the Lord. As a result they fell dead, and the only ones who waited to catch them were those who took their bodies out to be buried (Acts 5:1–10). These were two people in the church who believed in Greed Theology, and their misguided belief cost them their lives.

In the case of Saul, he fell on his face in fear because the glory of God, a light from Heaven, "shined round about him," and the clear voice of Jesus Christ thundered out to him, "Saul, Saul, why persecutest thou me?" (Acts 9:3–4). I would have fallen on my face (not my back), too! Of course, Saul wasn't healed of any ailment. Instead, he was smitten with blindness.

What we must keep in mind is that these worldly entertainers—and that's all they are—who put on their shows before audiences of people who may have sincere and urgent needs are there to take your money and manipulate you as any other hypnotist will do. I know. I have been taught to hypnotize people as a counseling therapist. I choose not to do so because I do not believe anyone should surrender his or her will to another person. That is the easiest way to come under the domination of Satan. But, then, this is, after all, the underlying goal of the greed preacher.

I once watched a professional hypnotist perform before a high school group. He used students as his objects. I noticed that he dismissed youngsters from the program who could not be hypnotized. It turned out that they were all Christian teenagers who would not yield themselves to demonic influences.

The rest of the students caved in to every suggestion the hypnotist gave. One student was told that there was a bomb in the auditorium and that upon a given signal she would desperately try to warn the audience, but she would not be able to speak English. She gave a prime example of speaking in tongues as they are used in today's churches. I watched as she ran around the auditorium (as I have seen spell-bound people do in Charismatic churches), leaping over students who were seated on the floor, and shouting in perfect charismatic tongues.

Another female student keeled over and became rigid when she was told that she was a board—similar to the trance that one who is "slain in the Spirit" goes through. In this case, the hypnotist placed the girl's neck on the back of a chair and her ankles on the back of another and stood on her mid-section. After all, she had become a board!

These illustrate the power of suggestion that even a greed preacher is able to use in manipulating his or her followers.

I do not mean to suggest that Christians should never conduct their worship in physical ways. Our Lord has given illustrations and encouragement to exhibit such expressions of devotion to Him. In 1 Timothy 2:8, we are instructed by the Apostle Paul, "I will therefore that [*the*] men pray every where, lifting up holy hands, without wrath and doubting."

Years ago, I attended the Founders' Week Conference at Moody Bible Institute in Chicago. William Culbertson was the President of the Institute at the time. He closed the conference with a powerful message from the Scriptures, but when he ended his sermon he did something that was completely foreign to his manner of worship—being, as I recall, an Episcopal bishop. With tears on his cheeks, he lifted his hands in the air and announced, "Friends, I feel strongly that the Lord wants me to raise my hands and worship Him. You may not feel the same way, so you are dismissed. You are certainly free to remain if you choose." No one left the auditorium, and many raised their hands as they prayed. To my knowledge, they had never done this before. There was no noise—just a softly-spoken reverent worship.

In the churches of the greed preachers, you would commonly see arms flailing in the air, bodies swaying back and forth or bobbing up and down. There would be a vocal uproar—many speaking in tongues or moaning in mass confusion. I have seen people running at break-neck speed around the auditorium as though the devil were chasing them. I've seen people dancing a jig in the aisles, and young women on their knees at the "altar" pulling their hair and moaning. In 1 Corinthians 14:33 we are reminded that, "God is not the author of confusion, but of peace."

Demonstration for the sake of demonstration is not the activity of sincere Christian believers. In fact, it is an expression of vanity and exhibitionism, an attempt at showing others how "spiritual" they are.

When a true believer responds physically to a deep, heart-felt love for the Lord, the emphasis is never on the demonstrative behavior but on the overwhelming sense of God's presence—an act of reverence and keen awareness of His sacrificial and infinite love. Tears may be shed, and joy may be felt, but the intention is not to show off.

We see an example of such spiritually-motivated physical expression in 1 Chronicles 29:20, "And all the congregation blessed the Lord God of their fathers, and *bowed down their heads*, and worshipped the Lord." It's so simple, yet so meaningful. That's the kind of expression that receives God's attention. After all, it is *His* attention that we should seek and not the attention of other people.

There is another example of a physical expression of worship given in the Scriptures. Paul said in Ephesians 3:14–15: "For this cause *I bow my knees* unto the Father of our Lord Jesus Christ, of whom the whole family in heaven and earth is named."

What was the *cause* that brought him to his knees? Paul continues in verses 16–17, "That he would grant you, according to the riches of his glory, to be strengthened with might [*power*] by his Spirit in the inner man; That Christ may dwell in your hearts by faith."

What was the result Paul was praying for? In verses 17–19, he added, "that ye, being rooted and grounded in love, may be able to comprehend with all saints what is the breadth, and length, and depth, and height; and to know the love of Christ, which passeth knowledge, that ye might be filled with all the fulness of God."

Paul concluded by placing the glory and honor where it belongs: "Now unto him that is able to do exceeding abundantly above all that we ask or think, according to the power that worketh in us, unto him be glory in the church by Christ Jesus throughout all ages, world without end" (20–21).

The healer's ability to induce people to humiliate themselves by going through the process of being "slain in the Spirit" is part of the hypnotic process that enables him to gain the kind of control over the seekers' minds that opens their purse strings.

Beware of those who have such a craving for wealth, and don't allow yourself to be wooed into following their example. When one loves money, his money breeds power, power breeds the pride of life, the pride of life breeds the lust of the eyes, and the lust of the eyes breeds the lust of the flesh—a fatal combination. That's why we are given this warning: "Love not the world, neither the things that are in the world. If any man love the world, the love of the Father is not in him. For all that is in the world, the lust of the flesh, and the lust of the eyes, and the pride of life, is not of the Father, but is of the world. And the world passeth away, and the lust thereof: but he that doeth the will of God abideth for ever" (1 John 2:15–17).

Paul graphically explains what happens to those who allow the desire for power and the lust for money rule their lives: "For the love of money is the root of all evil: which while some coveted after, they have erred [strayed away] from the faith, and pierced themselves through with many sorrows" (1 Timothy 6:10).

The Devil in the Works

He that committeth sin is of the devil; for the devil sinneth from the beginning. For this purpose the Son of God was manifested, that he might destroy the works of the devil. **[1 John 3:8]**

It seems strange that the scam artists—the false prophets in the churches of the last days—claim to have *all* of the spiritual gifts that the Bible says are imparted as the Holy Spirit sees fit. Before the Apostle Paul explains this, he exhorts us in 1 Corinthians 12:1: "Now concerning spiritual gifts, brethren, I would not have you ignorant." And yet, that is precisely what the greed preachers want you to be!

In 1 Corinthians 12:4–11, we are clearly told that God *divides* the gifts of the Spirit making sure that not everyone has all of the gifts: "Now there are diversities [*distinctions]* of gifts, but the same Spirit. And there are differences of administrations [*service*], but the same Lord. And there are diversities of operations [*putting into effect*], but it is the same God which worketh all in all.

"But the manifestation of the Spirit is given to every man to profit withal. For *to one* is given by the Spirit the word of wisdom; *to another* the word of knowledge by the same Spirit; *To another* faith by the same Spirit; *to another* the gifts of healing by the same Spirit; *To another* the working of miracles; to another prophecy; *to another* discerning of spirits; *to another* diverse kinds of tongues; *to another* the interpretation of tongues. But all these worketh that one and the selfsame Spirit, *dividing* to *every* man severally [Greek: *separately*—as a private assignment] as he [the Spirit] will."

The emphasis in these verses is on the *division* of the gifts to individuals so that the whole Church is actively engaged in the work of the gospel. Don't be confused by the KJV usage of the word *severally* because the original language actually means the opposite of our common usage. Even today's English dictionary defines *severally* to mean *distinct* or *individually*. It refers to the *individual* or *separate* assignment of each gift. It would be utter chaos if everyone had all of the gifts. It would also open the door to oppression or over–lordship by those who claim to have all of the gifts.

In verses 28–30, Paul ranks the gifts of the Spirit in order of importance in building and maintaining the Church, the Body of Christ, and reminds us that not everyone has the same gift: "And God hath set some in the church, first apostles, secondarily prophets, thirdly teachers, after that miracles, then gifts of healings, helps, governments, diversities of tongues. Are all apostles? are all prophets? are all teachers? are all workers of miracles? Have all the gifts of healing? do all speak with tongues? do all interpret?"

Of course, we also have the problem of some who would create their own "spiritual gifts." I once heard a pastor remark from the pulpit, "God has given me a special ability to understand the Scriptures." His intention was to quash any opposition to the outrageous diatribe he was about to launch in his sermon. So he simply created his own gift! When that happens, it is no longer a work of God but of the devil.

So, too, is the preacher who stares into the television camera, producing a show that will be aired days or weeks later, and declares that God has given him a "word of knowledge" that someone has a physical ailment God is healing at that very moment. In order to do that, he must decide for himself just what constitutes a "word of knowledge," Then he must be *prophetic* in order to complete his word of knowledge in the future *healing* of the person he has become magically aware of. By spiritual osmosis he has scanned the viewership through magic cameras, knowing all along there is bound to be someone out there who has the infirmity he has *discerned* and who will, therefore, assume he or she was the object of his discernment. That's where the TV greed preacher announces that the person must call in and speak with a counselor who will explain how to get healed. That's also when the counselor will encourage the unsuspecting seeker to send in money and sow his or her seed—because it's only through sowing a seed that one is able to receive his or her *miracle*.

Notice the spiritual gifts in operation through one person—the word of knowledge, prophecy, healing, and discernment. Never forget the admonition given to us in 2 Corinthians 11:13–15: "For such are false apostles, deceitful workers, transforming themselves into the apostles of Christ. And no marvel; for Satan himself is transformed into an angel of light. Therefore it is no great thing if his ministers also be transformed as the ministers of righteousness; whose end shall be according to their works."

Of course, all of this is rendered moot by the fact that several of these gifts are no longer in operation due to the fact that there will be no more special revelation. For example, if the Holy Spirit were to speak through a person today, whether it be in tongues, or interpretation of tongues, or any prophecy that is not already found in the Bible, then those words are just as inspired as the Bible itself and could be added to the Biblical text! That would be absurd. It would only add to the list of cultists like Jim Jones, Mary Baker Eddy, Charles T. Russell, Joseph Smith, and a host of other cult founders.

We are warned at the completion of God's written Word to mankind, in Revelation 22:18–19, "For I testify unto every man that heareth the words of the prophecy of this book, If any man shall add unto these things, God shall add unto him the plagues that are written in this book: And if any man shall take away from the words of the book of this prophecy, God shall take away his part out of the book of life, and out of the holy city, and from the things which are written in this book."

In Matthew 7:15–20, Jesus warns against such false prophets: "Beware of *false prophets*, which come to you in sheep's clothing, but inwardly they are ravening wolves. Ye shall know them by their fruits. Do men gather grapes of thorns, or figs of thistles? Even so every good tree bringeth forth good fruit; but a corrupt tree bringeth forth evil fruit. A good tree cannot bring forth evil fruit, neither can a corrupt tree bring forth good fruit. Every tree that bringeth not forth good fruit is hewn down, and cast into the fire. Wherefore by their fruits ye shall know them."

Then he tells us what will happen, and why, to these false prophets in verses 21–23: "Not everyone that saith unto me, Lord, Lord, shall enter into the kingdom of heaven; but he that doeth the will of my Father which is in heaven. Many will say to me in that day, Lord, Lord, have we not prophesied in thy name? and in thy name have cast out devils? and in thy name done many wonderful works? And then will I profess unto them, I never knew you: depart from me, ye that work iniquity."

There are three claims these false prophets make for themselves. First, they say they have prophesied in Christ's name. The Greek word for *prophesy* has three basic meanings: to *foretell events*, to *divine* (that is, to guess or make a conjecture), and to *speak under inspiration*. These people claim to foretell events beyond the scope of Scripture. For example, when I was a young Christian such a prophetess took me by the hands and prayed for me. Then she said, "*God told me* He is going to do great things through you. He is going to use your hands to heal many people." That was false prophecy because she claimed to receive direct revelation from God beyond the framework of the Scriptures. Of course, I can safely say, now that I am in my seventies, her prophecy was not fulfilled. Anytime a person claims to speak under inspiration from God, he is saying that he receives special revelation from God. That is Biblically invalid.

The second claim made by the false prophets in Matthew 7:22 is that they have cast out devils in Christ's name. The most common activity among today's false prophets is to cast out demons —assuming that *every* illness and trial is the result of demon possession or oppression.

Years ago, my wife and I had a daily radio program that was preceded by a popular Charismatic preacher who conducted a call-in prayer request segment. A lady called to complain about a painful toe as the result of getting out of bed in the middle of the night without turning on a light and banging her foot against the nightstand.

The pastor pressed his lips against the microphone and commanded the "demon of the toe" to come out of the woman. The fact is that I have never heard a greed preacher who didn't cast demons out of a host of people who clearly had other ailments. These preachers see demons in every corner!

The third claim made by these false prophets is that they have done wonderful works in Christ's name. The word *wonderful* is the Greek word *dunamis.* It means *great power.* It is where we get the words *dynamite* and *dynamo*. In other words the false prophets boasted that they had accomplished mighty and powerful deeds in the name of Jesus Christ. It is true that they always toss the name of Christ around freely, but it is almost always used to puff their own names, and always used to increase their wealth. I would never question their integrity if they had said, "Christ has done great and powerful works as we serve Him." But notice that every "claim to fame" they make is: "*We* have done," and they merely made use of His name in order to advance their "ministries." Their claims are, "*We* have prophesied in thy name; *we* have cast out demons in thy name; *we* have performed great and powerful works in thy name."

Of course, Christ will respond, "I never knew you: depart from me, ye that work iniquity." Iniquity is another word for sin.

You must be aware of the fact that every believer has direct access to the throne of God through Jesus Christ our Lord. We don't need a healer's touch because we can ask God personally for our needs. The same is true for special miracles. There are no apostles today because every apostle had all of the gifts of the Holy Spirit and were personally appointed by Christ. No one has received such an appointment since the Apostle Paul and perhaps Barnabas (Acts 14:14).

The opening verse in this chapter is a warning to be on the lookout for the false prophets who claim the works of the devil to be the manifestations of the Son of God through His Holy Spirit. When they do this, it is sin, and if it is sin, it is of the devil: "He that committeth sin is of the devil; for the devil sinneth from the beginning. For this purpose the Son of God was manifested, that he might destroy the works of the devil" (1 John 3:8). The Holy Spirit does not do the works of the devil!

Code Words or God's Word?

***Then Peter said, Silver and gold have I none; but such as I have give I thee: In the name of Jesus Christ of Nazareth rise up and walk.* [Acts 3:6]**

Notice that in the above Scripture verse, there are no gimmicks, no showmanship, and no props. It was a simple gesture on the part of the Apostle Peter who saw a man in need and offered to meet his need with a special gift, a gift from the Lord Jesus Christ. There was no money involved, no material object—just a word from the heart and an offer of a helping hand. "I don't have any money," he said. "The only thing I can offer is this: In the name of Jesus Christ of Nazareth, rise up and walk."

The man had asked for money or food. Instead, he received a new life. Peter took him by the hand, lifted him up, and a man who had never walked from the day he was born received instant strength in his ankles and feet and sprang to his feet and walked. Not only so, but he rushed into the temple walking and leaping and praising God. It's interesting, too, that Peter never asked a thing from the man in return.

When the people saw what had happened, they were amazed. Seeing their reaction, Peter asked them, "Ye men of Israel, why marvel ye at this? or why look ye so earnestly on us, as though by our own power or holiness we had made this man to walk?" (Acts 3:12).

Then in verse 16, he said, "And his name through *faith* in his name hath made this man strong, whom ye see and know: yea, the *faith* which is by him hath given him this perfect soundness in the presence of you all."

In other words, Peter disavowed any credit for the healing. His response to the crowd was, "We didn't do it. Jesus did through the faith He imparted to this man. His faith in Christ has made him whole."

Then Peter took wise advantage of the situation and delivered an invitation to them to be saved. "Repent ye therefore, and be converted, that your sins may be blotted out, when the times of refreshing shall come from the presence of the Lord; and he shall send Jesus Christ, which before was preached unto you" (19–20).

Typically, when anyone in the Bible is healed, it involves the salvation of that person or those who witness the healing.

How different was the lame man's experience from those who claim healing or the gift to heal today! I recently turned the television to a greed theology preacher who was in the midst of announcing that he would send a "prayer cloth" as a "point of contact" to those who needed healing. In other words, in order to be healed or receive a miracle, they had to have something to touch. I suppose the preacher was insinuating that without this point of contact, God would not honor their simple faith.

It's nothing new. So-called healing evangelists for decades have offered pictures of magic carpets to lay on your lap as you prayed, handkerchiefs, phony pieces of "the cross," supposed tear-stained rags, jewelry, and any other object that was prayed over or said to be touched by someone with the gifts of healing and miracles.

The healer in question went even farther to the point of being idolatrous. During his program (*Trinity*

Broadcasting Network, Breakthrough with Rod Parsley, June 9, 2005), he had what I would call a commercial in which a woman testified to the powers of her prayer cloth. She had wrapped her "last six dollars" in her prayer cloth, prayed over it, and as a result she got a new job, new car, and new house. She declared that it was the rag, not the Lord, who answered her prayers. She said, "I absolutely know that the breakthroughs that have happened in my life are because of *the prayer cloth* and *the anointing* that was upon *it.*" In other words, the prayer cloth had become an idol for her. However, apart from the Old Testament tabernacle and its contents, God never anointed *things* in the Scriptures. He anointed *people.*

You might say like the woman in Mr. Parsley's commercial, "But I held a cloth in my hand as I prayed, and my prayer was answered." But if you think for one minute that the cloth answered your prayer, you are worshiping the wrong god! Remember what James said in James 5:14–15, "Is any sick among you? Let him call for the elders of the church; and let them pray over him, anointing him with oil in the name of the Lord." Now, notice what comes next. "And *the prayer of faith shall save* [Greek: *save, deliver* or *protect*] *the sick*, and the Lord shall raise him up; and if he have committed sins, they shall be forgiven him."

Neither the oil nor the anointing with the oil healed the sick. It was the prayer of faith. The oil had no restorative power or any other power in it. The power rested in the grace of God through the prayer of faith.

God does not need a point of contact, be it a prayer rug, a drop of oil, or a slap of the preacher's hand, to heal people. In fact, the term *point of contact* is never used in the Scriptures.

You might ask yourself, "Do *I* need a crutch for my faith? Can my prayers be answered by faith without holding a handkerchief or paying a preacher?" Doesn't James say that "the effectual fervent prayer of a righteous man availeth much?" (James 5:16).

Either Christ is your only intercessor in prayer, or you have no intercessor at all! No man or woman on earth has greater power than Jesus Christ, and certainly no piece of cloth or trinket. Your prayers are always answered as a result of your faith—and faith alone! Anything else is an idol, whether it be a man or an object. Why do greed preachers offer gimmicks, such as prayer cloths or anointing oil, to sell (what they call sowing your seed), when faith alone is all that is needed? Why do they claim these objects are anointed? Why? Because if, as they claim, they possess a special anointing by God and can pass their anointing onto those objects or people, then they have the power to possess the minds and purse strings of all those who buy into their gimmickry.

Those who use the term "the anointing" speak as though it were a spiritual *gift*, but it is not mentioned in Scripture as a gift of the Holy Spirit. The only "anointing" the Scriptures mention for believers is the baptism of the Holy Spirit that occurs at the very moment we confess Christ as our Lord.

Since Christians are baptized, or filled, with the Holy Spirit from the moment of their confession of faith in Christ, there is no need to be anointed because we are *filled*! (See 1 John 2:20, 27; 3:23–24; Romans 8:9–17.) The Spirit of God indwells us to do all of those things that the so-called "anointing" is said to accomplish, and all Christians already possess all they need to accomplish God's will for their lives. I have yet to hear anyone define what constitutes a spiritual anointing beyond the *fulness* of the Spirit of God, and if you have that fulness, what more could some further anointing do? I have enough to accomplish anything God wants me to accomplish. What more could I ask for? (See Philippians 4:19.)

That brings us to another code-word used by today's false prophets. That is the word "breakthrough"—a word with no definition. It is never used in the Bible. Why would God use a meaningless word in *His* Word?

I suppose the notion of a breakthrough springs from the old expression *praying through*, another meaningless term. I grew up in a Pentecostal church that believed in "praying through" to receive the Holy Spirit with the evidence of speaking in tongues. Of course, there is no reference to *praying through* in the Bible either.

To *break through* carries the inference that there is a barrier between us and God until we reach the point of breakthrough. According to this viewpoint, that's when our prayers are finally heard. The problem with that is that there are no barriers that need to be broken through between God and His children—ever!

Romans 5:1–2 gives us this assurance: "Therefore being justified by faith, we have peace with God through our Lord Jesus Christ: By whom also we have *access* by faith into this grace wherein we stand, and rejoice in hope of the glory of God." We can't have peace with God if we don't have the assurance that He hears and answers our prayers. That's why we are promised *access* to Him.

John said in 1 John 5:14–15, "And this is the *confidence* that we have in him, that if we ask anything according to his will, *he heareth* us: And if we *know* that he hear us, whatsoever we ask, we *know* that we have the petitions that we desired of him."

Did you notice what was missing from those verses? Our confidence is not secured by any special anointing, neither are our prayers answered by struggling for a breakthrough. We *know* for a certainty that God hears and answers our prayers because we have access to Him by faith.

If Jesus Christ is your Lord, you don't need any breakthrough of any kind. You have the Holy Spirit indwelling you. He provides access to the throne of God through the shed blood of Jesus Christ and in the name of Christ. The Scriptures tell us that even when we don't know what to say the Spirit of God speaks on our behalf. Romans 8:26–27 tells us: "Likewise the Spirit also helpeth our infirmities: for we know not what we should pray for as we ought: but the Spirit *Himself* maketh intercession for us with groanings which cannot be uttered. And he that searcheth the hearts knoweth what is the mind of the Spirit, because he maketh intercession for the saints according to the will of God."

Rod Parsley, a bombastic charismatic electronic preacher brought several of the "health and wealth" code words together in one sweeping statement on his July 11, 2006, *TBN* show, *Breakthrough*, when he said, "Our *Breakthrough* prayer warriors are here to *believe with you* for your miracle *touch* from the Lord." He continued. "Let faith-filled *breakthrough* prayer partners *agree with you* for your every need to be met in Jesus Christ."

This example illustrates a major flaw in the electronic preacher syndrome: It places too much power, too much authority, on mortal men and women and assumes or steals too much from Almighty God. When the flesh gets control of "religion," it makes a mockery of the truth which rests in Jesus Christ.

The priest who requires his parishioners to confess their sins to him has robbed God of *His* authority. "If we confess our sins, *he* [our Lord Jesus Christ] is faithful and just to forgive us our sins, and to cleanse us from all unrighteousness" (1 John 1:9). "For there is one God, and one mediator between God and men, the man Christ Jesus" (1 Timothy 2:5).

The man or woman who tells you that you can only receive your "miracle" or "breakthrough" by way of his or her "anointing" and his or her "point of contact" has robbed God of His divine nature by assuming what belongs to Him. Who should the one in need run to for help—the preacher or God?

A young woman once told me, "Oh, God [the profanity she learned from the preacher], you should have heard Brother Smith. You should see the miracles he works—all the people he heals!" Never once did she mention the name of our Lord, apart from her profane use of it. While the preacher may say that God does the work and that he (the preacher) is just the instrument, he knows full well that he is getting the credit for whatever takes place in the eyes of his followers. He can throw his shoulders back, puff his chest out, and say to himself, "Ain't I great? And just think of all the money I get for this." Jesus never asked for or accepted a penny for His ministry. Let a man argue that "it costs a lot of money to be on television and radio, have my own Bible college, and print all of my literature. I have to ask my 'partners' to help me pay for all of that."

I've got news for that nitwit. God doesn't need television, radio, Bible colleges, or printed material to accomplish His will. He uses *people* like you and me to spread the gospel of Jesus Christ and to help those who need help, and if we can afford to do it through the media, well and good. Otherwise, we can simply tell people about God's love. That's why God gave us our tongues.

Every gospel "show" that I have seen on television is broadcast from a multi-million dollar church complex or "headquarters." They range across denominational lines, and they all demand multiplied millions of dollars in order to continue their ministries each year.

Some make a great display of showing off the majestic, costly pipes and organs, along with the pomp of ceremonial marching choirs and large orchestras. The cameras scan the facilities as if to say, "Look what we've got! The Lord sure has been good to us!" Others show off their crystal cathedrals and football arena-sized structures. I wonder what would happen if someone could break into their broadcasts with pictures of starving children, decaying corpses lying on cracked, dry ground, and other desperate situations. I guess in some instances they are brash enough to do that themselves, and people are naive enough to ignore the wasted money on all of the pomp and assume that it takes it all to raise the money that may or may not go to help the needy. In reality, most of it is designed to get you to sacrifice your hard-earned paychecks to create their own high-rolling lifestyles, and every electronic preacher that I have seen is a multi-millionaire. Why would anyone send his hard-earned money to make a rich man richer?

How many people could be sent out to tell others about Christ if the $20 million annual television budget of one preacher were given to that kind of ministry? When you throw in the other TV ministries, you might have as much as $500 million to apply to *real* soul-winning ministries, as well as helping the needy and assisting missionaries. The fact is that very few people get saved through the media. The vast majority are saved in churches and personal soul-winning ministries.

Remember, Peter didn't have any money to give to the begging lame man. Instead, he gave the lame man new life in Jesus Christ—and he didn't ask for a penny in return! Neither did he make a great public plea for people to "sow their seed" to his ministry. The simple fact is that the gospel doesn't cost anything, nor does the love that every Christian must exhibit. If we expect other people to pay for everything we set out to do for Jesus, where is the sacrifice that the Lord demands of us? Are we placing a price on Jesus and on His message of hope—the hope of glory?

The Commercialization of the Church:

***And [Jesus] said unto them that sold doves, Take these things hence; make not my Father's house an house of merchandise.* John 2:16**
***It is written, My house shall be called the house of prayer; but ye have made it a den of thieves.* Matthew 21:13**

What does it cost to have someone pray for you? What does it cost, apart from the blood of Jesus Christ, to have your sins forgiven? What does it cost to receive God's blessings in your life? The answers to these questions have already become clear in this book, but let's take a second look in the context of Christ's confrontation with the moneychangers at the entrance to the temple.

We find the incident recorded in John 2:13–16: "And the Jews' passover was at hand, and Jesus went up to Jerusalem, And found in the temple those that sold oxen and sheep and doves, and the changers of money [*money-brokers*] sitting: And when he had made a scourge of small cords, he drove them all out of the temple, and the sheep, and the oxen; and poured out the changers' money, and overthrew the tables; And said unto them that sold doves, Take these things hence; make not my Father's house an house of merchandise."

When Jesus entered the temple in Jerusalem, He discovered men sitting at tables collecting money from the people as they came seeking purification. These men were telling the folks who came that they could only have atonement by filling the moneychangers' pockets with whatever worldly possessions they had. I can imagine the words they used: "If you buy my doves, or my oxen, or my sheep, you can be blessed by God. The more you give for them, the greater will be His forgiveness and blessing." Or, perhaps, using modern vernacular, they came straight out and said, "You can also pay cash. See, we have boxes of money that has been contributed. God will see your generosity and forgive you and pour out His blessings upon you." Perhaps they might have said, "Ours are the best sacrificial doves in town, and God expects the best from you. After all, they have been anointed and are now your point of contact."

Sound familiar? During Marilyn Hickey's Spring, 2006, TBN television programs, she and her daughter, Sarah Bowling participated in a ceremony with their fellow greed preachers, Oral and Richard Roberts in which they poured what I assume to be olive oil over their hands and into a large bowl. The women then offered the oil, which was placed in tiny vials for sale to people who wanted God's blessing either for healing or making money, giving the impression that having had the oil poured over *their* hands turned it into a magic potion. This probably falls under the category of an "anointing" of the oil or perhaps even a "point of contact." The Hickey/Bowling mother and daughter team continually offer special items—gimmicks—on their TV show (*Marilyn and Sarah Today*) to lure their viewers into sending them their hard-earned money or perhaps pitiful Social Security checks.

Today's moneychangers sell cross pendants, tiny mustard seeds imbedded in glass or plastic beads, trinkets of wood cut from "olive trees in the Holy Land," rags that have been prayed over, paper "prayer rugs," specialty Bibles, books, recordings, and countless other items. Now, understand. There is nothing wrong with selling many of these things, but when it is couched under the guise of exchanging gifts with the promise of gaining influence with God, it is sin! In other words, the false prophet tells you, "Sow your seed of $100.00 to this ministry, and I will send this anointed pendant as my gift to you. When you hold this in your hand and pray, God will give you a breakthrough to your miracle. He will also return to you a hundred-fold of what you have sown [in this case $10,000.00]. He will bless you in 'good measure, pressed down, and shaken together, and running over.'" As we have already seen, such a snatch of Scripture is always taken out of context and used to rip off the listener.

In the case of the money changers at the temple, our Lord became so angry that he made a whip, or scourge, of small cords and drove these evil men out of the temple, saying, "It is written that My house shall be called a house of prayer, and you have turned it into a den of thieves" (Matthew 21:13). Then he turned over the tables of money, scattering the ill-gotten gains across the floor, all the while flailing at the thieves with his hand-made whip.

God will do the same to the thieves who pretend to be ministers of the gospel today. These are the ones of whom our Lord said, "Many will say to me in that day, Lord, Lord, have we not prophesied in thy name? And in thy name have cast out devils? And in thy name done many wonderful works? And then will I profess unto them, I never knew you. Depart from me ye that work iniquity" (Matthew 7:22–23).

The four people on the *Marilyn and Sarah Today* show that I just referred to have boasted the same boasts, and I am convinced they will find themselves wanting in the eyes of our Lord Jesus Christ.

The charlatans of Christ's day, "the chief priests and the scribes and the chief of the people, sought to destroy him" (Luke 19:47). They were incensed that He took their authority away, their means of gaining great wealth, and their only solution was to think of violent ways to do Him in.

"Tell us by what authority doest thou these things? or who is he that gavest thee this authority?" they demanded (Luke 20:2).

Jesus replied that, if they would tell him by whose authority John the Baptist baptized, then He would answer their question. The chief priests, scribes, and elders didn't want to admit to John's high calling, but they were afraid of the people, so they refused to answer. Jesus said, "Neither tell I you by what authority I do these things" (Luke 20:8).

These religious leaders faced the same issues as the last-day Laodiceans do. Their pride was on the line. Up to that point they were in charge; they had the authority—the power. They were the ones who had authorized the presence of the moneychangers, and they were the ones who received most of the money, much like it was with the United Nations whose leaders had made themselves rich on the "Oil for Food" program in Iraq. But now Christ has assumed control, and those in charge of the moneychangers saw their own power slipping.

In Luke 20:46–47, Jesus said, "Beware of the scribes, which desire to walk in long robes, and love greetings in the markets, and the highest seats in the synagogues, and the chief rooms at feasts; Which devour widows' houses, and for a shew make long prayers: the same shall receive greater damnation."

The pride of life and the love (or lust) for money were bringing them down into damnation or judgment at the hand of God. Not only so, but they had become thieves and cutthroats, stealing the sacrificial offerings of the poor who thought they had no other access to God's blessings. They were exactly like those in our churches today who proclaim their own power to heal and call down Heaven to deliver the helpless. "And by the way," they add, "if you really want God's blessing, you'll have to sacrifice your money. Then God can bless you a hundred times over. Trust me. He will," and the new moneychanger walks away snickering over the naive victim he has lured into his scam, counting his fistful of dollars, and mumbling, "Ma-ma-ma-ma-pa-pa-pa-pa," pretending to pray in an unknown tongue.

Perhaps you are thinking, *I'm sure glad those things don't happen in my church*! But I'm not so sure that is true, knowing the direction America's churches are taking today.

I drive past a local church near my house that uses a large pink figure of a hog on its front lawn to advertise a public sale of barbeque pork steaks and brats. That particular church does this almost every weekend. The money was supposed to be taken in to meet the budget of the church. It doesn't sound like a major offense, but it does represent a potential step in the wrong direction. If we become reliant on fundraising from the community, where does it stop? This seems backward. Instead of giving to the community as a testimony for God, we are expecting the community to give revenue to us.

Another fund-raising approach has been around for as long as I can remember. It takes the form of a gambling enterprise called Bingo! It has proven to be as addictive as any other form of gambling.

There is a more recent means of fund-raising that turns the church property into a commercial enterprise. It consists of renting spaces for commercial sales of products. The rental fees go to the churches, and the profits go the individual salesperson or business. At what point does the church cross the line from ministry to moneychanging? It could be interpreted as a lack of faith in God's ability to provide for his Church.

Perhaps the worst form of fund-raising the churches have borrowed from the world is the most common—the carnival! These sleazy traveling con artists set their tents, rides, and concessions up on church property to lure people, including unsuspecting children, into gambling their money on rigged activities that leave no room for anyone to win anything. But as long as the wicked church meets its budget, so what?

The fact is that the only Biblical way to support the various ministries of the local church is through the freewill giving of its congregation. You see, the church belongs to God, not the general public. The members of the church are responsible for meeting the financial needs of the church. The church is not called to make merchandise of itself. That's exactly what the moneychangers were doing when Christ overturned their tables of greed! What's wrong with trusting the Lord to meet the needs of the church? After all, Philippians 4:19 assures us that "my God shall supply all your need according to his riches in glory by Christ Jesus."

You see, there is no difference between the preachers of greed and the churches who choose to rake money from the local citizens through various sales gimmicks. God didn't call those local citizens to build churches. He called His own people to give according to their means! And if that giving doesn't meet the budgetary requirements of the church, then the church is living beyond its means! It simply doesn't need what the leaders think it needs. Do something innovative! Cut the budget! Forgo some of the trappings that make the members more comfortable or make the building—especially the sanctuary—more aesthetically attractive.

Your church doesn't need expensive equipment to show pictures on the wall or the words to songs your congregation doesn't know—nor for that matter—even wants to know. Here's a new idea! Use your hymnals! Then the members of your congregation can return to *harmonizing*—since they will actually have *music* to follow!

The problem we face with today's churches is the result of wrong thinking. People think that a church is not successful unless it has a wall-to-wall membership, or is at least filled with bodies—saved or unsaved. That way, a preacher or deacon can complain that we need a bigger sanctuary, and our offerings aren't big enough. One preacher invested his church income in a sports stadium. Now he can show it off on television and claim to be a successful personality—the kind that Jesus will tell, "Depart from me ye workers of iniquity. I never knew you."

We have finally reached the days that Jesus warned us would come—the days that would be like those of

Noah and Lot. Let me repeat, the Apostle Paul alerts us to this time in 2 Thessalonians 2:1–2, "Now we beseech you, brethren, by the coming of our Lord Jesus Christ, and by our gathering together unto him, That ye be not soon shaken in mind, or be troubled, neither by spirit, nor by word, nor by letter as from us, as that the day of Christ [Greek: *day of the Lord*] is at hand. Let no man deceive you by any means: for that day shall not come except [or until] there come a falling away first." That's when the man of sin, that son of perdition—the antichrist—will be revealed.

We are presently experiencing that "falling away" [Greek: *apostasia* or apostasy] on the part of our American churches, and many other places in the world. The telltale signs that give them away include the commercialization I have referred to, the brevity of the preaching of the Word, the worldly music that has captivated the souls of our congregations, and the constant introduction of so-called new Bible versions—not translations from the Hebrew and Greek texts, but rewriting the Scriptures to fit the writer's viewpoints. In other words, they are little more than commentaries on the Bible. Just because a preacher or teacher can stand before an audience and declare what he is reading to be the Word of God doesn't make it so.

These are all issues that should be a warning that the spirit of antichrist is invading the Church. I don't care if the words to the songs in the church sound religious or otherwise acceptable. One can easily tell by the gyrations of the musicians and the applause they receive that their music is for entertainment purposes only and not to honor the Lord Jesus Christ. The music is being used entirely to draw people into the church, saved or unsaved, not to get them saved, but to get them into the pews. The applause will make the entertainers think they are future superstars—and perhaps put money into their pockets. The preacher, of course, will think that he is gaining recognition by his affiliated churches. That most assuredly will guarantee him a bigger church with a bigger salary later on. You can usually recognize these phony gospel musicians and preachers by their appearance and often, by the fact that you may not be able to understand their words—words that are drowned out by the noisy instruments. I must confess that this is probably a blessing in disguise!

It's time for Christians to 'fess up and admit they are moving in the wrong direction. Quit wasting the money that should be given to strengthen the gospel message in a world that has flatly rejected Christ and all He stands for. Forget the excitement of the world's music, the golf course, your favorite television show, or whatever diverts your attention from the Word of God and the worship that our Lord expects from us. It's time to return to holiness and devotion to our Lord. Get serious, and stop fooling around with what was meant to be Christ-honoring worship.

We should follow John's example and pray "even so come Lord Jesus" from the depths of our soul with a sense of expectancy and joy, taking our minds off the dollar sign and placing it in the hope of glory.

Like it or not, most Christian people are no different from the rest of the world's masses. They are allowing themselves to be manipulated by their own desire to be like everybody else. As a result, they translate the word *want* to mean what the seed crowd calls *need*! They disregard Paul's admonition to be content with what God has supplied.

After all, God does know what is best for us—and the best is yet to come!

About the Author

Larry D. Rudder is a graduate of Southern Illinois University at Edwardsville, Illinois with a B.A. in History and Government, and an M.S. ED and S.D. in Counselor Education. He is also a graduate of Moody Bible Institute and studied Bible at Wheaton College.

He began preaching at the age of 18 and has conducted revival and evangelistic meetings across the country for over fifty years. He has written a number of gospel songs and recorded them with his wife Jeanette, while Dove award winner Henry Slaughter produced and played the keyboards for the recordings.

He is the author of *Christ at the Dinner Table, Christ in All His Glory, The Way of the Cross,* and two focus books: *The Great Confession* and *Selling Jesus.*

www.ingramcontent.com/pod-product-compliance
Lightning Source LLC
Chambersburg PA
CBHW031519040426
42445CB00009B/299
9781932060195